INDEXING, THE ART OF

INDEXING,
THE ART OF

A guide to the indexing of books and periodicals

by

G. NORMAN KNIGHT, MA

Barrister-at-Law
Late President of the Society of Indexers

With a Foreword by the
Rt Hon. HAROLD MACMILLAN, OM, PC, FRS

Absente auxilio perquirimus undique frustra,
Sed nobis ingens indicis auxilium est.

Without a key we search and search in vain,
But a good index is a monstrous gain.

London
GEORGE ALLEN & UNWIN
Boston   Sydney

First published in 1979
Reprinted 1980

GEORGE ALLEN & UNWIN LTD
40 Museum Street, London WC1A 1LU

© The Executors of G. Norman Knight, 1979

Index © The Executors of G. Norman Knight, and Anthony Raven, 1979

British Library Cataloguing in Publication Data

Knight, Gilfred Norman
    Indexing, the art of.
    1. Indexing
    I. Title
    029.5   Z695.9   78-40882

    ISBN: 0-04-029002-6

Typeset in 11 on 12 point Garamond
and printed in Great Britain by Unwin Brothers Limited,
The Gresham Press, Old Woking, Surrey

Dedicated to

THE SOCIETY OF INDEXERS

*from many of whose members I have received
considerable help in compiling this book*

CONTENTS

FOREWORD

by the Rt Hon. HAROLD MACMILLAN, OM, PC, FRS

Twenty-one years ago, when I was "somewhat occupied with
other matters", I was glad to send a message of encouragement to
the Society of Indexers upon its foundation. The Society has now
come of age, and its President has taken the opportunity to pass
on the wisdom derived from its two decades of experience, and
from his own eighty-six years, to write what must surely prove
to be the definitive work on the art of the index. For indexing is
indeed an art – wherein the fashionable machinery of the computer
may be a useful slave but must never become the master – and it
requires the highest degree of intelligence and skill in those who
practise it.

A good index can be much more than a guide to the contents of
a book. It can often give a far clearer glimpse of its spirit than the
blurb-writers or critics are able to do. What could better epitomize
the richness and variety of, say, North's Plutarch, than this?

> Eagle how many eggs she layeth, 439. two fought over Brutus campe,
>   1067
> Earthquake at Lacedaemon, 503
> Ebrus flumen, 591
> Ecclesiastical persons exempted from warres, 307
> Eclipse of the Moone, 555, 976. of the Sunne, 619

Or the salutary realism of Michel de Montaigne than such an
entry as, "Age as imperfect as youth in vertues", which I fear even
my fellow octogenarian the author of this book must admit to
having a grain of truth.

Or of the whimsical serendipity of Norman Douglas's *Together*
than his observation upon poets?

> Poets, should avoid towns, 82; generally born naked, 165;
>   talk nonsense about pomegranates, 202

Douglas, of course, is too ready with his jokes. Nevertheless, every good index should have a joke. But one is enough. And if it can conclude the work, so much the better, as in T. E. Lawrence's *Letters*, where we read:

Zulus, misunderstood by Oxford dons, 108. *See also* TATTOOING

But I must not multiply instances. Mr Knight has made his point with a list of excellently chosen or contrived examples in this book. In one of them I find myself in the noble company of Macgillicuddy's Reeks and the Machine Gun Corps. If, as Bernard Shaw is alleged to have said, an index is a great leveller, I am glad to see that in this instance at least I have enjoyed that levelling upwards which has always been the aim of the Conservative Party.

December 1977

AUTHOR'S PREFACE

It may be objected that this book is on the whole rather elementary. But this has been so arranged deliberately, because any indexer who observes all the elementary principles will not go far wrong, while sometimes advanced indexers are apt to make their own rules. My aim has been to provide authors in particular who find themselves bothered by their publisher's rule that the author is responsible for providing an index, with the necessary information.

I wish to acknowledge my gratitude to the publishers for their considerable patience in waiting for the completed manuscript of a book that was commissioned more than seven years ago.

I also wish to thank most cordially the Rt Hon. Harold Macmillan, OM, PC, FRS, for his kindness in contributing a Foreword.

I also wish to acknowledge the great helpfulness I have received from John Gordon, the Secretary of the Society of Indexers, and in particular from my friend Russell Stevens, who voluntarily undertook to type a great part of the book to my dictation, as well as being responsible for many helpful hints and suggestions. I also wish to thank the publishers' editor, Mr Anthony Raven, for the very great trouble he has taken in preparing the manuscript for the press; he has made a number of useful suggestions and has helped me to revise and bring up to date parts of the book that were originally written some years ago. Mr Raven has also very kindly shared the compilation of the index, which I was unable to complete owing to the state of my health at the age of eighty-six.

G.N.K.
June 1978

INDEXING, THE ART OF

CHAPTER ONE
Introductory

*A full index is added, without which no publication beyond
the size of a pamphlet can be deemed compleat.*
John Noorthouck (1746–1816),
Preface to Grand Lodge *Book of Constitutions* (1784)

The Latin word "index" had the meaning: "he who, or that which,
points the way". It became fully anglicized in the sixteenth century,
by the end of which it had acquired its literary sense. Thus we find
in Marlowe's *Hero and Leander* (1593), Sestiad II.129:

> Therefore, even as an index to a book
> So to his mind was young Leander's look.

But at that period, as often as not, by "an index to a book" was
meant what we should now call a table of contents. This is shown
in the often quoted passage from Shakespeare's *Troilus and Cressida*
(1603), I.3.344:

> And in such indexes, although small pricks
> To their subsequent volumes, there is seen
> The baby figure of the giant mass
> Of things to come at large.[1]

But the real importance of this passage is that it establishes for all
time the correct literary plural; we can leave the Latin form

---

[1] Shakespeare's plays have four other allusions to "index" in this sense: "As index
to the story we late talk'd of" (*Richard III*, II.2.148); "The flattering index of a
direful pageant" (*Richard III*, IV.4.85); "Ay me, what act, That roars so loud, and
thunders in the index?" (*Hamlet*, III.4.52); and "an index, and obscure prologue to
the history" (*Othello*, II.1.257).

"indices" to the mathematicians (and similarly "appendices" to the anatomists).

The earliest indexes

It is sometimes thought that the earliest index (in the correct meaning of the word) to an English book is that to Alexander Cruden's *Concordance* (1737), but there had been earlier examples, often called "tables". H. B. Wheatley instances Sir Thomas North's translation of *Plutarch's Parallel Lives* (1595) – a book of which Shakespeare made full use for his classical plots. Again, Scobell's *Acts and Ordinances of ... Parliament* (1658) is "An Alphabetical Table of the most material contents of the whole book", preceded by "An index of the general titles comprised in the ensuing Table".

Even Cruden had been preceded by a number of Jewish authors. For instance, in 1691, according to M. Z. Barkai, Shmuel ben Alexander published an index to the legal book *Hoshen u-mishpat* with the explanation: "these keywords simplify locating the point for which the judges are searching".[1]

"Index" defined

Of the inconsiderable number of textbooks that have been written on the subject of indexing only two, so far as I am aware, attempt to define an index. H. B. Wheatley[2] states: "An index is an indicator or pointer out of required information". The other is from Mary Petherbridge's *The Technique of Indexing* (1904), a book which is not very highly regarded today. It defines an index as "a summary of all statements and allusions contained in a book", which is clearly too wide and otherwise unsatisfactory. Fuller and better is the definition in the British Standard:[3]

---

[1] "Indexing in Israel", *The Indexer*, Vol. 8, No. 1 (April 1972), p. 6.

[2] Henry Benjamin Wheatley (1838–1917), *What is an Index?* (1878). His far better known *How to Make an Index* (1902) has long been out of print but is still one of the most useful works on the subject. He was one of the founders of the Library Association in 1877 and founded the Index Society. His great index formed Vol. 9 of his edition of *The Diary of Samuel Pepys* (1899). The Library Association's annual Wheatley Medal (see Appendix 5) was named after him.

[3] This document, *Recommendations [for] the preparation of indexes to books, periodicals and other publications* (BS 3700: 1976), published by the British Standards Institution, is a revised version of the original British Standard on indexing, BS 3700: 1964. 1976 and 1964 are, of course, the dates of publication.

A systematic guide to the location of words, concepts or other items in books, periodicals or other publications. An index consists of a series of entries appearing, not in the order in which they appear in the publication, but in some other order (e.g. alphabetical) chosen to enable the user to find them quickly, together with references to show where each item is located.

John Askling ("What is an Index?", *California Librarian*, March 1951) has a definition into which he tries to introduce some of the aspects of compilation:

An index is a classified subject analysis of the content of a book, books in series, or of periodicals or pamphlets wherein the entries and sub-entries are each set down in correct subject form; all entries being alphabeted in one alphabetic order by standard rules.

This definition could stand and shine but for the vitiating use of the word "classified" (by which Mr Askling probably means nothing more than the grouping of subheadings), for in an alphabetical index there should be no classification (see Chapter 5). Each indexable subject should have its own individual entry. If a system of classification were to be carried far enough (to its illogical extreme) the result might be only one entry, which would be the subject of the book itself, and all the contents would follow in the form of classified sub-entries, sub-sub-entries, sub-sub-sub . . . *ad infinitum*.

Components of an entry

The unit of an index is the *entry*. This comprises the *heading* together with any qualifying phrase (*qualification* or *modification*) and at least one page reference number (*references*) or "see" *cross-reference* (see Chapter 5); and also, where the references are numerous or distinctive enough to demand systematic grouping, *subheadings* are used, forming, with their appropriate references or cross-references, *sub-entries*. Thus, to take two very simple examples:

Greek (modern) words, transliteration of, 41
Scientific journals, indexing of, 104–5
    "Standards" for, 103, 148

In the above entries, "Greek words" and "Scientific journals" are the headings; "(modern)" is a qualification; "transliteration of" and "indexing of" are modifications; while "Standards for" is a subheading and, combined with its references, forms a sub-entry. In a sense subheadings may be regarded as modifications.

The primary purpose of an index is to indicate the location of any particular item. It serves two classes of user: the researcher who seeks to find what (if anything) a book has to say on some subject in which he is interested; and the reader who, having read the book, wishes to refresh his memory of some topic. Both classes must be constantly borne in mind by the indexer. "An index is as good as its users think it is", declared Dr John Rothman, Editor of the *New York Times Index*.

What publications should be indexed

If the quotation that appears at the head of this chapter is somewhat all-embracing, at any rate John Noorthouck was erring on the right side. Any "publication beyond the size of a pamphlet" would include books of plays and poems as well as fiction, although none of these is normally indexed. But I must not be too sweeping, for it must be remembered that since 1790 at least five concordances have been compiled for the works of Shakespeare, while the 38th volume of the Windsor edition of those works contains an excellent index to all the Notes in the entire series. Then, in the matter of poems, some years ago a competition was mooted among certain enthusiasts of the newly formed Society of Indexers to provide the best index for T. S. Eliot's "The Waste Land". Moreover, there is very commonly an "Index of first lines" in books of poems.

It is the question of novels that presents the greatest problem. Samuel Richardson, who has been called the first true English novelist, was persuaded by his friend, Dr Johnson, to publish (in 1755) in the form of a volume of 410 pages an *index rerum* to *Pamela*, *Clarissa* and *Sir Charles Grandison*. Today in the case of most novelists it would smack of presumption if one of them were to add an index to his new novel (although surely not so heinous an offence as is committed almost daily by serious writers who allow their works of non-fiction to be published with no index[1]).

---

[1] Malcolm Muggeridge once described a book without an index as "like a railway timetable not giving the names of the stations". Yet his own collection of random pieces, *Tread Softly for you Tread on my Jokes* (1966), was produced without one.

But it was not so regarded when George Gissing provided an index for his delightful *The Private Papers of Henry Ryecroft* (1903). Nor when Sir Alan Herbert ("A.P.H.") produced lengthy indexes to his *Misleading Cases* (1927), *Uncommon Law* (1935) and *Bardot M.P.?* (1964). Since the amazing trials narrated therein were never heard in any actual court of law, those books must certainly rank as fiction. A selection of A.P.H.'s wonderfully witty entries can be sampled in my final chapter. In America there have been published three indexes of science fiction magazines, one in 1952 (covering the years 1926 to 1951) and the other two, dealing with more recent magazines, at the end of 1968. Another great humorous writer, Lewis Carroll, insisted that all his novels should have indexes, with entries for the author's favourite jokes; while in 1971 the *Grand Prix* of the Académie française was awarded to Jean d'Ormesson's *La Gloire de l'Empire*, which usefully included an index, as did the English translation, *The Glory of the Empire*.

Great classical novels are those which most stand in need of indexes. There are already two separate *Dickens Dictionaries* (1872 and 1909) and a *Dickens Concordance* (1907), while Anthony Spalding's masterly *Handbook to Proust* (1952) was described in a leading article in *The Times* as "often a better companion for Proustians than Proust himself". To mark the centenary of the death of Robert Surtees, Robert Collison produced a useful *Jorrocks Handbook* (1964), consisting of an elaborate index to the characters and chief contents of *Handley Cross*, *Hillingdon Hall*, and *Jorrocks's Jaunts and Jollities*. The late Evelyn Waugh once related that he possessed a translation of Tolstoy's *Resurrection*, published in New York, which had "a particularly felicitous index". Likewise a librarian is known to me who has compiled a comprehensive index to John Galsworthy's *Forsyte Saga,* and there must be many other instances.

Students would undoubtedly welcome an indexed edition of a translation of *Don Quixote*, as also of the best novels of such classical writers as Sir Walter Scott, Jane Austen, the Brontë sisters, Thackeray and Trollope, or (nearer our own day) Hardy, Kipling, Meredith and R. L. Stevenson. Could not some enterprising publisher, when issuing reprints, take this need into consideration? The very *novelty* – the pun was unintentional – of the notion might induce an extra readership sufficient to cover the added expense.

Even novels produced as educational textbooks for exams containing a "set book", although fully annotated, (unforgivably) never include an index, in spite of the fact that such an adjunct might greatly assist the pupils who have to use them. These are editions of novels that should unquestionably be provided with indexes.

In the realm of non-fiction it is generally agreed by publishers, authors, critics and indexers alike that there are certain classes of book that *must* be indexed (but even in these fields there are frequent serious lapses). They include works of history, biography, belles-lettres, philosophy, religion, travel, geography, science (of every kind), law and medicine. Some of London's most prominent publishers contend that there are a number of "general" books to which an index is superfluous and a waste of money. The books for which most publishers seem to jib at providing indexes are the ephemeral light-weight reminiscences. But surely any book of reminiscences that is worth publishing at all is likely to be used as a reference-tool and therefore deserves an index. At any rate, a stinging rejoinder to the publishers' contention came from the pen of Alan Brien in a 2½-column article on "Indexes" in the *Sunday Times* (23 February 1969): "I suspect that the continued production of indexless books is simply due to a mixture of parsimony and slovenliness".

Encyclopaedias are in a class by themselves. Since in most encyclopaedias nowadays the articles relate to specific (as opposed to broad general) subjects and have their titles arranged in alphabetical order, their proprietors sometimes claim that an index is unnecessary. But of all works of general knowledge the encyclopaedia most requires an index. The fact that the subject headings are given in alphabetical order provides no clue to the host of other important topics dealt with, a great number of which recur under many more than one heading. This is recognized by the publishers of the best encyclopaedias.

Unfortunately the excellence of the twelve-volume *Everyman's Encyclopaedia* is sadly marred by its being indexless, as also is the otherwise admirable ten-volume edition of the *New Universal* (1948). The latter I possess and the frustration that can be caused is typified by one of my own experiences. In the course of indexing I had come across an allusion to "Uraniborg (the Castle of the Heavens)" in Denmark. The encyclopaedia yielded nothing about this in the article on that country or under "U", but eventually, after wasting much time in research, I ran it to earth under "B", where I found considerable enlightenment on the Castle of the Heavens in the article on Tycho Brahe, the Danish astronomer who owned it. But if only there had been an index!

In his masterly *Encyclopaedias: their history throughout the ages* (1964) Robert Collison sums up the position exactly: "The encyclopaedia is a poor tool without its index". There is still time for the *Everyman* to add a thirteenth volume. But whether a "Pocket Cyclopaedia" could afford the space for a worth-while index it is more difficult to say.[1] Possibly it would have to rank with Noorthouck's "pamphlet".

The question of the indexing of newspapers is dealt with in Chapter 9.

Qualities needed in an indexer

Once, when asked by a friend what I was doing, I incautiously told him I was compiling an index. He immediately exclaimed: "How can you waste your time and talents on such a simple task as picking out the proper names in the proofs of some book?" That reflects a common misconception. As will be seen in the chapters to come, far more is needed for the production of a good index, which is anything but a mechanical job. Wheatley came to admit that a good indexer must be both born *and* made.

In his informative contribution on "Indexing" to *Progress in Library Science 1965* (edited by Robert L. Collison), John L. Thornton lists the following "faculties of a born indexer – an orderly mind, infinite patience, and the ability to approach [the] book from the readers' angle". These are all important and I should feel disposed to add: first and foremost, common sense; also imagination, a general knowledge above the average, a good memory (during the "work-in-progress" stage) of relevant entries already made that may need cross-referencing or link of some sort, and finally an insight into the meaning of the author (that is, of course, when the index is being compiled by someone other than the author).

In such a case, indeed, there can scarcely be too great a rapport

---

[1] By means of using thinner paper, however, *The Pocket Encyclopaedia of Freemasonry* (1978) by Norman Knight and Frederick Smyth provides a useful index.

between an indexer and his author, and this can often be conveniently established by means of the telephone. It is my experience that nowadays most authors, even when disinclined to compile their own indexes, nevertheless tend to take an increasing interest in their progress and final quality. This brings us to the vexed question of the author-indexer.

The author as his own indexer

Many British publishers now include in their standard contract a clause requiring the author, if called upon, to provide an index, that is, either to compile the index himself or else to pay a professional indexer. This may lead to many an author's undertaking a task which he would not otherwise have attempted. In his admirable pamphlet *Making an Index* (3rd edn, 1963) the late Gordon Carey held the view that "*almost* any book *could* be indexed more efficiently, and with less trouble, by its own author than by anyone else".[1] It has, however, been disputed whether in fact the author is in every case the best indexer of his own works. It has been argued that the very fact of his all-embracing knowledge of his subject might sometimes prove a disadvantage in that he might assume a similar knowledge in the index-user and so might fail to select the headings sought by the user. Some have thought that few authors are temperamentally suited to making their own indexes.

This seems to be borne out in the case of the world-famous *Baby and Child Care*, by Dr Benjamin Spock, who insisted upon preparing the index himself because "an indexer would not understand the headings under which a mother was likely to look". But Mrs Hazel Bell, herself both a mother and an indexer, has complained in *The Indexer*[2] that when her new baby developed strange patches on its face, she was baffled by finding no help from any subheading under "face" or "skin" in the index. Also,

When I thought the child had swallowed a bead which might be lodged in its throat, it was astonishing to find nothing under "swallowed objects" – especially as there is an entry under "O" for "objects in nose and ears", but no "objects, swallowed". "Throat" only yielded "throat infections".

[1] The italics are mine. Mr Carey once assured me that a good many authors simply could not do the job.
[2] Vol. 6, No. 4 (Autumn 1969), pp. 181–2.

The child wasn't choking, but at last I assumed Dr Spock might assume a mother to think he was, and looked there; the "choking" entry led to a paragraph subheaded, "swallowed objects and choking".

However, it must be remembered that the first three of the Library Association's Wheatley Medals for outstanding indexes were won by author-indexers. It is a fact that "some of the best indexes to books have been produced by their authors – and some of the worst. The truth would seem to be that, *provided he is willing to master the technique*, the author can be the ideal indexer of his own works."[1] Many books requiring indexes have more than one author and then, of course, the hiring of a professional indexer will usually be necessary.

Indexers anonymous

At one time, indexers suffered from an enforced anonymity. Apart from those rare instances where an author saw fit to acknowledge the work of his indexer in the book's preface it was virtually impossible to discover who had compiled the index to a particular work.

But the British Standard (BS 3700: 1964), following in this respect the earlier American standard for indexes (1959), laid it down that "for any substantial index, the qualified indexer, no less than the illustrator or any other collaborator, should be given proper credit by name in the publication indexed". "Substantial index" is assumed to imply one of not less than sixteen columns.

Advantage of this recommendation is at present being increasingly taken, although of course it is still within the indexer's province to choose that he does not wish his name to appear. But if he does wish it and the publisher should raise objections, he is advised to call the latter's attention to the BS clause I have quoted. No longer need indexers be, like alcoholics, anonymous.

The most suitable place for the credit by name is immediately below the index title:

INDEX
Compiled by ——

[1] Introduction to G. Norman Knight (ed.), *Training in Indexing* (1969). (Italics in original.)

The privilege can sometimes prove to be double-edged. In the words of a witty clerihew in *The Indexer*:[1]

> it is only right
> For the publisher to print the indexer's name
> So he can take any praise (*or blame*).

I once had personal experience of the parenthesized part, in which the italics are mine. In 1958 I was commissioned to index the 800-page history of a famous opera house. As far as one is ever satisfied with one's own efforts, I felt fairly satisfied with this one, which met also with the decided approval of both author and publisher. Several reviewers of the book mentioned the index, all but one favourably. Thus Sir John Squire referred to "the admirable index of this book", while the critic of *The Musical Times* spoke of "44 pages of the finest index I have ever come across in any book of this type".

The exception was a well-known music critic who was noted for his drastic castigation of the books entrusted to him for review. Aware of this reputation and anxious to forestall such treatment of his work, my author had astutely invited him to read the proofs of the text, which he did. Thus deprived of his natural prey, the critic vented his vituperation upon the unfortunate indexer, to whose effort he devoted no fewer than twenty-five damning lines, possibly a record amount of space to be bestowed on the index in an ordinary book review. He even descended to personalities: "The name of the compiler . . . is printed at the head of his index; one of the White Knights, I fancy?"

The above is an example of how publicity can recoil in the hands of a captious critic. But such instances are believed to be rare.

How many indexers for one work?

The option of taking credit for an index, when exercised, also allows it to be seen how many hands have been at work in the compilation. Thus, the single index to *Progress in Library Science 1965*, referred to above, is shown to have had two compilers, although it occupies only eight pages and the whole book has but 216. This happens to be an index of reasonably high standard,

[1] Vol. 5, No. 1 (Spring 1966), p. 22.

but in general the practice of collaboration in indexing an average-sized book is not recommended. One reason is that consistency and uniformity of treatment, which are so essential for a good index, are apt to be lost when there are two or more directing minds. (Collaboration is quite distinct from the employment of assistants, who can be extremely useful in the checking of page references and other similar tasks.)

I have only thrice been persuaded by publishers to find collaborators, on each occasion when working under great time pressure. The first concerned the making of a 92-page index to the 1,274-page text of a history of architecture. Here I chose two collaborators and, the sections of the book seeming to divide themselves naturally, the result was moderately successful. But not so with the second, a four-volume work on Association football. Here I had one collaborator (alas! now deceased), who had a certain reputation as a technological indexer, but he cannot have taken this particular task very seriously. When I found that he had indexed a section with the heading "A Great Day for the Rangers" under G (not for Glasgow but for Great), and that there was no relevant entry under Rangers, all his cards had to be completely overhauled and little (if any) time was saved after all.

This shows how important it is that, whenever there is a joint effort, one of the collaborators shall be responsible for co-ordinating the combined work and for its final form.

It is even more important in the case of giant indexes, such as the whole-volume ones to the larger encyclopaedias or to great legal works like Halsbury's *Laws of England* (in forty-two volumes), where a whole team of indexers has inevitably to be employed. Here there must be an indexer-in-chief or index-editor, and it is suggested that he should not participate in the actual work of indexing.

How many indexes for one work?

Wheatley was a stout campaigner on behalf of "the index, one and indivisible". An index, he declared, "should not be broken up into several alphabets". This assertion may be regarded as somewhat over-dogmatic, for there must be exceptions. A legal textbook, for instance, requires as a rule a Table of Cases cited (in alphabetical order) and a separate Table of Statutes (in chronological order), neither cases nor statutes being included in the general index. Again, an anthology, if furnished with a general index, may reasonably need a subsidiary index of first lines of poems. (An American anthology, *Poetry of the English Renaissance*, edited by J. W. Hebel and H. H. Hudson (1929), by the use of typographical distinctions very effectively combined in a single index what might have been separate indexes of authors (capitals and small capitals), titles (italics), and first lines (ordinary roman type). But I should have preferred the first lines to be enclosed in quotation marks.) Also, when a book or periodical contains advertisements it is desired to index, they must be given a separate alphabet.

When, a few years ago, a disputation had arisen in the columns of *The Indexer* on the topic, "One Index or More than One", the late Gordon Carey, then President of the Society of Indexers, stepped in with a neat analogy:

> Surely the question "Should a book have more than one index?" is no more controversial than, say, "Should cricket be played in one sweater or more than one?" As in the latter case the obvious answer is, "It depends on the weather", so in the former it is, "It depends on the subject".

Ease of reference must be the prime consideration, and this is rarely served by having multiple indexes. Their danger is that the researcher may so easily become bogged down in the wrong index and, not at once finding the object of his search, may give up his quest in disgust. If an indexer is instructed to provide more than one index to any work, he should in the first of his preliminary notes (see pp. 165–6) at the beginning of each such index give a clear warning of the existence of the other or others.

In 1957 appeared a book on biblical archaeology which was thought to need no fewer than five indexes: (1) Modern Names of Persons, Societies, Institutions, etc. (76 entries); (2) Biblical Names of Persons, Tribes, Buildings, etc. (300 entries); (3) Biblical Place-names (357 entries); (4) Subjects (96 entries); (5) Biblical Passages (700 entries). These indexes (the whole five of them) are of un-exceptionable quality. But why this massive proliferation? I should have considered that the only topic that could possibly need a separate index was (5), although in a general index different typography (say, large and small capitals) could usefully be employed for the headings of (2) and (3) and its use explained in a preliminary note.

Today the chief offenders are those periodicals that persist in retaining separate indexes for Authors and Subjects. An author may very well be also a subject in the same publication, and it is annoying to have to consult two indexes to make sure of having found all the available information about him (or her).[1]

It is believed that multiple indexes must have been first introduced in imitation of the system of classification in use in library catalogues. But then, although they have some rules in common, indexing and cataloguing are entirely distinct arts. After all, if large encyclopaedias, with their vast diversity of material, can be content with but one index apiece, why cannot lesser publications? As Sir Edward Cook pithily put it in his well-known essay on indexing: "Multiplication of indexes is an unmitigated nuisance."[2]

The length of indexes

The length of an index depends on a number of factors, of which the length of the text may be the most obvious. The character of the book is also important: whether it is an academic work for which a very detailed and thorough index is desirable, or a "light" work for which a simpler index may suffice. Clearly, the length of the index will depend on the number of names and other indexable subjects contained in the text, and on the desirability of providing subheadings (on which, see Chapter 3). Experienced indexers learn to assess the probable length fairly accurately, but even the most experienced are sometimes taken by surprise when a particular book proves to need more, or fewer, entries than seemed likely to be the case.

Generalization has its hazards, but provides a useful base for some tentative conclusions. Some useful research on this subject was undertaken by Mrs Margaret Anderson and published in *The Indexer*.[3] Reckoning by the number of lines in the index expressed as a percentage of the number of lines in the rest of the book – a page of two columns each of fifty lines counting as fifty lines of index – Mrs Anderson's findings were as follows.

Most of the indexes of a number of recent books on history were

---

[1] I have been asked by a scientific indexer of high repute to make an exception – which I gladly do – in favour of major scientific journals, in whose indexes subjects might easily be swamped by the vast number of authors.

[2] "The Art of Indexing", from his *Literary Recreations* (1918).

[3] Vol. 5, No. 1 (Spring 1966), pp. 3–4.

in the range of 5 to 8 per cent of the text. Biographies tended to be more lightly indexed than history, and were more likely to have no index. Out of twenty-two biographies examined, sixteen had indexes in the range of 1 to 4 per cent, with a tendency towards increasing length in the more recent books. Of the remaining six, four had indexes between 5 and 6 per cent, while two had unusually long indexes, 9·7 and 9·5 per cent respectively. Geographical works varied a good deal. Discursive books describing travel or a particular district mostly had indexes in the 2–5 per cent range. Those of two histories of exploration reached 5·3 and 6·2 per cent. The length of indexes in science books was more clearly related to the difficulty of the text. Books for general readers, and for sixth-formers and first-year undergraduates, mostly had 3–5 per cent indexes. For more advanced textbooks, 6–8 per cent indexes were usual, often in three columns in books on medicine and chemistry. At the top of the scale were some very large, highly specialized books, with two-column indexes as long as 15 per cent of the text. Some annual reviews of the sciences also had (three-column) author and subject indexes amounting to 15 per cent.

The length of an index is, of course, no criterion of its usefulness. But since nowadays a *good* index is increasingly regarded as an important part of a book or periodical, the indexer deserves to have every facility, in the matters of the time and space allotted, for the production of just such a one. Of all systems of information retrieval the index is the simplest and (provided it be a good one) the most reliable.

CHAPTER TWO
The Mechanics

Drudgery divine
Rev. George Herbert (1593–1633),
The Temple (1633)

We are sometimes assured that before embarking on the preparation of an index it is necessary to read through the whole of the text two or three times. This does not, of course, apply to an author-indexer, who is already fully aware of his book's contents. For the professional indexer it is a counsel of perfection. If he is to make sure of providing a properly balanced index, it is certainly essential that he make a preliminary study of the text sufficient to get a grip of the book's feel and structure. Whether the recommended procedure is always practicable depends on two factors: (a) the form in which the text is presented to the indexer; (b) the time he is allowed in which to complete his task.

Time and space

If the indexer is commissioned early enough, he may have the luck to induce the author to lend him a spare copy of the manuscript, which he will have plenty of time to study while the original copy is being printed; should the MS have numbered paragraphs, he may even start indexing. It is more likely, however, that he will have to wait for the proofs before he can insert the page references. If the proofs arrive in the form of galleys, again he will have time for a preliminary reading while they are being corrected. But most publishers now look upon ordinary galley pulls as old-fashioned and insist upon the printer's supplying *paged* galley proofs in the first instance, sometimes for only part of the text. If the page proofs of the complete text are sent all together, everything will depend on the time allowed for the index's compilation, a subject which sometimes causes a difference of opinion between the publisher and the indexer.

At one time it used to be complained that, coming last in the book, the index came last also in the publisher's thoughts and sometimes proved even an afterthought. Now that publishers have become more index-conscious, this is no longer true as a general rule, and sufficient time is usually allotted for the making of the index, having regard to the length and complexity of the book. But more often than not it happens that some link in the tight schedule snaps – perhaps the author is late with some of his copy or there may be delays on the part of the printer or the proof-reader. There may then be an attempt to repair the schedule and make up the lost time by taking it out of that allocated for making the index.

An instance is on record of an indexer's being offered over the telephone on a Thursday afternoon the compilation of an index to a historical work of some 300 pages, to be completed during that week-end! Such pressures ought to be resisted. It is the provision of insufficient time, or of inadequate space, that is responsible for some of the unsatisfactory indexes that are still to be encountered today.

If insufficient space is available for the index, this may not be due to the publisher's lack of appreciation of the need for an index, or to his inability to assess the kind of index that is required. In his calculations before sending the typescript of a book to the printer, the publisher normally allows enough pages for the kind of index that seems to be called for. (It is often helpful if the indexer himself can be consulted at this stage.) But, for a number of reasons, the text when proofed may turn out to be a little longer than was expected. It may be only a matter of a page or two, but that can pose very great problems for an indexer who had been expecting, perhaps, only eight pages. (The opposite problem, too many pages, is less troublesome, since one or two blank leaves can be left at the end of the book, while it may also be possible to insert a half-title for the index or appendixes, or to make other adjustments.)

Faced with insufficient pages, the indexer must exercise all his ingenuity in eliminating unnecessary items. It is sometimes helpful to deliver an index that is over-length, but with "optional cuts" marked that would, if absolutely necessary, reduce it to the required length. This alerts the publisher's editor to the importance of the material that is in danger of being deleted, and may encourage him to persuade the designer to make adjustments elsewhere, so as to avoid the need to shorten the index after all.

Only as a last resort should the indexer ask for more pages to be made available, as the expense may be considerable. Because books are printed on large sheets each of which, when folded a number of times, makes (usually) sixteen pages, and, as an absolute minimum, four pages, it stands to reason that, with the best will in the world, the publisher cannot add a page or two to accommodate an index that is slightly over-length. Publishers will think very hard before going to the expense of adding four pages that have not been budgeted for, especially if the indexer needs only another page, or half a page.

Cards and slips

Compiling an index necessitates the preparation of a number of entries, which in their final form must be either typewritten or very legibly handwritten in ink. Several different methods of recording them are in use, but probably 90 per cent of indexers today use either index cards or "slips".

Both can be treated here together, since their uses are so similar. Whichever kind is employed, they must all be of uniform size in one particular job. Cards, which should be thin, can be readily obtained from a stationer or (more cheaply) can be specially cut by a printing concern. The size usually preferred is 5×3 in. Slips can also be obtained from a printer to the indexer's choice of size, ranging from 8×4 in. to 5×2 in., or they can be home-made from fairly stiff paper; a quarto sheet, folded twice, will provide four slips, each $8 \times 2\frac{1}{2}$ in.

Two further kinds of equipment are essential. The first is a container in which to hold the cards (or slips) while in use on one's desk. For this a wooden tray, with sides shallower than the slips or cards, is best; its suggested length can be about 18 in. and it must be broad enough to accommodate the chosen width of the slips or cards. But many experienced indexers continue to make do with the traditional shoe-box with shortened sides. As the anonymous ballad-maker wrote in *The Indexer*:[1]

> O bring to me ten thousand cards
> And my brave shoe-box too.
> An index I must make to-night
> Fast as a man may do.

Cheap containers can, in fact, be adapted from any suitable boxes obtained from friendly stationers, sweet shops, etc.

The other necessity is at least twenty-four guide-cards, marked (on a projecting surface) with the letters of the alphabet – X, Y and Z on the bought version usually come together on the same guide-card. Alternatively, stationers' shops will supply metal markers to be affixed to the tops of blank cards, with tiny slips of paper to be inscribed with the letters and inserted in their windows; their use can be extended to alphabetical sub-divisions, e.g. Co, Cr, Cu, etc.

No card or slip should contain more than one entry. If the sub-headings are too numerous for one card, then the heading must be repeated at the head of the second and any subsequent card to preserve its alphabetical order in the holder, but must there be ringed round (if the cards themselves are to be sent to the printer), otherwise it may appear in the proofs. The second and subsequent cards should be given ringed numbers and may conveniently be kept in the tray in reverse order, (3), (2), (1).

It is recommended that cards or slips be kept in alphabetical order, that is between the appropriate guide-cards, throughout the indexing process. In this way they can be readily referred to at any time and subheadings or fresh references can be added. It has long been my practice to use cards rather than slips and to *type* on them all headings and subheadings and the first reference in each case, adding any further references in ink. Cards stand up well in the tray and they can be used again, twice or even three or four times – in which case, of course, the entries for the various indexes must be clearly distinguished, e.g. by the use of different coloured inks.

Some indexers prefer, in the interests of speedy indexing, to use a new card or slip for each item as they come to it, and to keep the cards in their original page order until they have checked all the references with the page numbers on the text proofs. This practice

---

[1] Vol. 5, No. 4 (Autumn 1967), p. 206.

involves not only a great waste of stationery but also a considerable time spent at the end in sorting and editing the cards and reducing their number, so that what is gained on the swings of speed at the start is lost on the roundabouts of sorting and editing.

The page (or paragraph) references are a vital part of any index and, ideally, their accuracy should always be carefully checked, when making the index and when correcting the index proofs. But I fear it is a rule more honoured in the breach than in the observance. As Tom Tatham has suggested in *The Indexer*,[1] if ever the Society of Indexers were to have occasion to call upon its members to "work to rule" (which God forbid!), this and the "rule" already mentioned about having to read through the text several times before starting the index, would be enough of themselves to cause the requisite frustration and delay.

Continuous sheets of gummed labels

Another method of recording entries is by the use of gummed sheets of paper (obtainable at any large stationers), perforated throughout their length at intervals of two or three inches. I have no personal experience of this system, which has been described by Robert L. Collison in *The Indexer*.[2] Each item is written or typed on its own perforated strip. When the indexing is completed, and the "entries have been checked with the text" (but see the preceding paragraph), the strips are separated at their perforations and sorted alphabetically. A certain amount of editing will also be necessary to eliminate repetition of headings, duplication of references, etc., and then the gummed strips are mounted on quarto rough paper, ready for the printer. There is naturally a wastage of stationery since it is preferable to make fresh entries for every page reference to the same heading rather than go back through the gummed strips to trace the first mention of that heading. Against this there is the speed gained by the use of continuous stationery.

I can see the system's coming into its own if a printer were to refuse to accept a collection of cards or slips. I have never heard of any such refusal, although a printer does sometimes complain of their being "rough copy", for which he may charge more.

---

[1] Vol. 6, No. 1 (Spring 1968), p. 12.
[2] "Indexing at Speed", *The Indexer,* Vol. I, No. 1 (March 1958), pp. 7–13.

The gummed label method has its uses also in the indexing of periodicals, "afterthoughts occasioned by the contents of succeeding issues being easy to insert since the slips are not separated until the current volume is completed".

Metal-flanged leaves

In the same article Collison calls attention to an elaborate system which can be very useful for those indexes – e.g. for standard yearbooks and directories – which do not require very extensive variations from year to year. Here it is possible, unless the index is a very large one, to put all the entries on

> a visible index consisting of a series of metal-flanged leaves, bearing on each side cellophane-covered stiff strips which slip into slots on either margin. This is a most flexible type of index, for each side of each metal leaf will hold up to 200 entries, and insertions and withdrawals of individual entries can be made immediately, provided the column is not completely full.
>
> The entries are written or typed on perforated sheets of paper or thin cardboard and are only separated when ready for sorting and insertion. The metal leaves can be supported on stands or supplied in folding form for desk work, and each leaf can be detached – a point which makes the index more mobile. As against the comparatively high initial cost of this equipment, subsequent expenditure is limited to renewal of stationery, since none of the parts is likely to wear out or need repair.

Thumb-indexed notebooks

The use of a notebook – preferably loose-leaf – is one of the earliest methods of recording the entries for an index. Indeed it has been described as "primitive". I used it in some of my early indexes and found it completely satisfactory for a short, simple index of, say, six to eight pages. But the consensus of opinion among experienced indexers is that it lacks the flexibility of cards or slips and that it could not be expected to work well for a large index, or one involving many sub-subheadings.

It is now sometimes called the Stallybrass System after an indexer whose description of its use for a twenty-column biographical index heralded a symposium in *The Indexer*.[1] Mr Stallybrass seemed unaware that he was reviving a well-tried method of indexing and thought he might be accused of heresy.

[1] Vol. 6, No. 1 (Spring 1968), pp. 4–13.

He bought an ordinary stiff-backed notebook of 200 pages for 4s. 3d. – the requisite number of cards would have cost 22s. – and, taking his cue from the number of pages allotted to each alphabetical sub-division in the index to *Chambers's Encyclopaedia*, marked the notebook's recto pages accordingly, reserving the verso pages opposite for emergency interpolations. Thus the nine pages for B were: B–Bap; Bar–Baz (ignoring Baq); Bea–Bem; Ben–Bez; Bi–Bl (there being no references to the *Bhagavad-Gita*!); Bo; Bra–Bri; Bro–Buk; and Bul–By. Within each recto page he divided the space by guesswork, allowing for those entries that were likely to have sub-entries. He confessed to having had to revert to the use of cards for entries under the names of the biographee and the cognominal members of his family, together accounting for a fifth of the index.

Notebooks can be bought already marginally thumb-indexed, but they will probably be found not to be divided according to the indexer's needs, and in any case will lack alphabetical sub-divisions. It is suggested, therefore, that anyone wishing to try this system should obtain a loose-leaf notebook and, having decided on his sub-divisions, should mark the series of alphabetical combinations on tiny labels, which should project from the edges of the appropriate pages, being affixed to them by means of transparent sellotape. The first "A" label should protrude from the top right-hand corner, the remaining labels gradually descending to the bottom, so that all are visible at a glance. If the labels are too numerous, it may be necessary to have more than one series.

The advantages of the notebook method, which are also enjoyed by the "shingled sheets" method explained in the next section, are as follows: (1) compactness and portability of material; (2) speed of operation; (3) no risk of losing an entry.

The great disadvantage of both this and the following system, apart from their lack of flexibility, is that they inevitably require the typing of a fair copy before the index can be submitted to the publisher. But if this typing is done at home, it allows some of the editing to be done in the process.

Shingled sheets stapled together

While Oliver Stallybrass cannot claim to have invented the "Stallybrass System", credit for the origin of the "shingling" variant must be given to that well-known authority on indexing, Dr J. Edwin Holmstrom, who uses it himself and thus explains it in *The Indexer*.[1]

Foolscap sheets, which should preferably be lined or squared, are wire-stapled into batches of ten with their bottom edges shingled over one another about a quarter of an inch. In the bottom right-hand corner of each sheet are written the initial group of letters of whatever is to be the last word that may be indexed on that sheet. These markings, which serve the same purpose as those printed on the tabs of guide cards, are distributed in the right proportion of alphabetical range with the aim of ensuring that every sheet shall become about equally full. This is done from the successive pages (or from every nth page, n being suitably chosen) in some existing index or dictionary relating to the same sort of subject matter.

The entries are written in alphabetical order on the right-hand side (corresponding to the notebook's rectos) of the appropriate foolscap sheets, the left-hand side (corresponding to the versos) being reserved for the interpolation of any later entry that might otherwise have had to be excluded, however carefully the spacing has been arranged; the sheets can be delimited by folding them down the middle.

The chief disadvantage of this system is the practical one that constant lifting of the corners of the sheets tends to make them excessively dog-eared. But it has been effectively adapted for a year's cumulation of the index to a monthly journal.

A novel method

A somewhat unusual method was devised by Dr Lindsay Verrier, a resident in Fiji, for compiling the index to a book on those islands.

> I read through the book in galleys [he is lucky to be able to obtain unpaged galleys – see above] and underline in pencil words or phrases that need indexing, and so am ready for instant action as soon as the page-proofs arrive.
>
> Taking a foolscap sheet and two carbons into my typewriter, which is an elegant Olympia electric, I set margins for two columns, and write my index straight-out, in page order.

[1] Vol. 2, No. 1 (Spring 1960), pp. 26–30, and Vol. 4, No. 4 (Autumn 1965), p. 129.

I then take a rather large plastic bowl, one of those kitchen bowls with a snap-on cover, and shut the doors and windows and snip up the whole index into single-line pieces, which all fall into the bowl. The snap-on lid allows me to leave the work at any stage.

Next, I sort the small strips into first-letter order on a table, getting 26 piles of varying size, and when done stuff them into old envelopes which are rubber-banded together. Now, at leisure, and in the depths of the silent tropic night, the real work can begin.

I tip out the first ("A") envelope on a large smooth table, turn the strips face-up, and slither them into alphabetical columns. This is very easy and rather fun.

When a number have been done, I take a galley-sized piece of newsprint, torn from the large roll of 18-inch newsprint that is fixed on the wall, and run on to it two lines or strips of PVC adhesive from one of the standard dispensers. With tweezers the little strips can be picked up and touched-down on the PVC, to which they instantly and permanently adhere. . . . This pasted-up set can be corrected or amended in several ways: it can be written-on; new lines can be pasted on; it can be cut through and new segments inserted, and so on.

This operation gives me a line-by-line index that is a pleasure to copy. By counting the numbers one can type straight out across the page in two columns . . . This copy is discussed with the author, and the final copy made in single column to suit his wishes . . .

Typings are of course made with several carbons, to guard against disasters. . . . Our main enemies are hurricanes, housegirls and cocktail parties.[1]

"Rather fun", indeed, but the Verrier system involves typing out the entire index on three separate occasions.

In the foregoing sections six distinct media for the preparation of an index have been offered for the choice of the indexer. As Miss Delight Ansley, an American indexer, expressed it in the symposium already referred to, "The best way to make an index is the way that the indexer finds most convenient. If the result is a good index, nobody will care whether it was made with a notebook, a computer, or knots in a piece of string."

[1] Reproduced (with Dr Verrier's permission) from *The Indexer*, Vol. 6, No. 3 (Spring 1969), pp. 118–20.

CHAPTER THREE
Headings and Subheadings

The indexer should imagine himself the eventual reader and try to anticipate needs and expectations. Under what heading would he be most likely to look for information? How full should these headings be? Should they be expanded, modified, or broken down? What should be included? What omitted?

The Chicago *Manual of Style* (1969)

Having chosen what medium we are going to use for presenting our entries, the first stage in compiling our index starts; this is the selection of our entry headings, those guides to the information contained in the book or periodical being indexed. It is the most difficult part of the indexing process.

A heading, sometimes described as the "main heading" in contradistinction to its subheadings (which will be dealt with at greater length in a separate section), consists of the all-important *keyword* (or "catchword", as it is often called), i.e. the initial word of the entry, together with any qualification or modification, the whole being based on some item in the text. These, with the addition of a reference or references and any sub-entries, compose the entire entry, which may consequently occupy sometimes one line, sometimes several lines in the index.

If the heading consists of a single word, it is called a *simple heading*; if it consists of two or more elements (with or without connecting hyphen), it is called a *compound heading*. Some examples of compound headings are:

Amalgamated Union of Engineering and Foundry Workers
Bar Point-to-point
Labour Party, and African Federation
Underwater-to-air missiles

Compound headings often take the form of two nouns or noun expressions linked by the conjunction "and",[1] which in this context can have four quite different uses:

1) to mark an ordinary joint association, as in "Trinidad and Tobago" (where an ampersand might be employed), or "Smith, Ian, and his followers", or "Headings and subheadings";

2) to denote a widening of the concept by the second element of the heading, as in "Ships and shipping" or "Plants and plant life", or by the use of antonyms – "Sobriety and inebriety" – so long as both elements are treated together in the text: the second element should be entered as a *cross-reference* (see Chapter 6). This, so long as the two elements have sufficient in common, can be a useful device;

3) to indicate a mutual interaction between the two elements, as in "Science and religion", or "Government and the taxpayer";

4) with a modification, to express a view held by, or a statement made by, the first element, as in "Labour Party, and African Federation", or "Cutter, C. A., and the Schwartz rule".

In nearly every case, each element will need to be separately entered ("double entry"), or at the least to have a cross-reference.

The selection of headings can be done during a careful preliminary read-through (either of the whole book or of a particular chapter or periodical article) by underlining in the text any word or expression that the indexer considers a user is likely to look for in the index; he can further write in the margin of the text any wording he thinks ought to be added to what he has chosen, or any notes thereon.

Thus, to take an example from the paragraph which defines "Entry" in the text of the original British Standard on indexing (BS 3700: 1964):

2.2 **Entry.** A unit of the index consisting of a heading (and qualifying expression, if any) with at least one reference to the location of the item in the text or with a "See" cross-reference.

definition of
plural   pl.
refs. to items indexed, entries indexed
pl.

---

[1] The late Mrs E. M. Hatt ("Onery-Andery", *The Indexer*, Vol. 1, No. 3 (Summer 1959), p. 76) considered that and "can be too often used . . . Not too often for indexer's convenience, but too often for faithful reflection of authors' meanings".

Here the indexer's underlinings in the text prompt the recording of the following entries on the slips or other chosen medium:

Cross-references, 4.4
   "see", *see* "See" cross-references
Entries
   definition of, 2.2
Headings, 2.2
Qualifying expressions for headings, 2.2
References to items indexed,
    entries, 2.2
"See" cross-references, 2.2
Text indexed, the
   references to items in, 2.2

It must be pointed out that this example has a quite unusual number of indexable items; it is rare indeed to find so many in such a few lines. On the other hand, neither "unit" nor "location" nor "item" is underlined for entry. This is because it is thought that no index-user would normally look for any of them. The omission of "index" here is for a different reason; it is partly because it would scarcely be sought in this particular context, but also, and more importantly, because the whole pamphlet is concerned with indexes and, if the word were to be indexed every time it occurred in the text, the entry itself would become merely a vast, unwieldy synopsis.

As regards the seven selected entries listed above, the following points should be noticed.

1) The keyword of every heading is fitted with an initial capital letter. This is the old-established practice. But nowadays it is quite common practice (and indeed, as some indexers think, preferable) to confine the use of the initial capital letter to those headings where the keyword is itself a proper name.

2) In the entry "Cross-references" the purpose of making the subheading itself a cross-reference instead of giving it a reference number is explained on p. 56.

3) Several headings are put in the plural form although the items they allude to in the text are in the singular. This usage is explained on pp. 44–5.

4) Each subheading in the above list is only one of a number in every case in the corresponding entry in the actual index to BS 3700: 1964.

5) The term "Qualifying expressions", which forms the fourth heading, in BS 3700: 1964 comprises both "qualifications" and what are called "modifications" in these pages. (For the difference, see pp. 19–20.)

The keyword

The importance of the keyword ("Cross", "Entries", "Headings", etc. in the list) is twofold. First, it will be the word to be sought by the index-user and so should be chosen with the utmost care. Second, on it will depend the heading's order in the alphabetically arranged index.

The keyword should, as a rule, be an actual word in the portion of the text being indexed, for it is awkward to consult an index and then not to find the word, given there as the keyword, in the part of the text indicated. If, therefore, a synonym is deemed more desirable as the entry-heading, there should be a cross-reference from the actual text word. The question of synonyms presents problems and will be treated more fully in Chapter 5.

Easily the commonest part of speech for a keyword is the noun (including a verbal noun or gerund). But in many general indexes adjectives (including participles) do not lag far behind. Except in the index to a thesaurus or to some work in which special words are singled out for examination, an adjectival keyword should not form a simple heading; that is to say, it should always be immediately followed by the noun that it qualifies; also it should only be used when it forms a distinguishing part of the concept of the whole heading, or else is the first word of a well-recognized term, e.g.: "fictitious names"; "classical music"; "bitter beer".[1]

The indefinite article should never be used as a keyword except in an Index of First Lines: "A Book of Verses underneath the Bough". Such a heading as "An outing in Oxfordshire" is a symptom of indexing incompetence. The definite article, on the other hand, not only has its place in an Index of First Lines – fifty-five such entries start with "The" in *The Oxford Book of Victorian Verse* – but also can be used as a keyword when it forms

---

[1] But in a work concerned with brewing, "bitter" would well stand on its own as a substantive.

the first part of a proper name, e.g. La Fontaine, Jean de; Du Pontet, Godfrey; but not "The Hague" – see p. 86, below.

Adverbs should be used sparingly but, if sufficiently distinctive, can form effective keywords. Dr Holmstrom has a striking instance in his index to *The Sea* (1962):

Aerodynamically:
  rough flow,   81
  smooth flow, 80

Again, pronouns lack the precision needed in a keyword and are rarely used, except in indexing a title, e.g. Rider Haggard's *She* (1887), or *I, Claudius* (Robert Graves, 1934), or "Who's Your Lady Friend?" (song). In a general index the use of prepositions is only allowable in similar circumstances, e.g. "In the Interests of the Brethren" (Kipling). Not so long ago there appeared an index containing the heading "Without body murders". But who would be disposed to look under W for murders in which the victim's body had not been found? Surely, "Bodiless murders" would have been better. Similarly, conjunctions and interjections are

above parts of speech, however, occur quite often as keywords in indexes of first lines of poems.

The great thing is that the keyword shall be an expressive word, and one that is likely to be the object of the index-user's search. Thus, in a naval index "Destroyers" makes a better heading than "Torpedo boat destroyers", although the latter was the original official name; if both terms are used in the text, there should, if necessary, be a cross-reference – "Torpedo boat destroyers, *see* Destroyers". Similarly, "Computers" seems today preferable to "Electronic computers".

Singular or plural keywords?

Allusion has already been made to a noun keyword's being given a plural number in an index heading although used in the singular in some parts of the text. Where the noun appears in the same grammatical number throughout the text, the heading should of course be given that number. But often the same noun is used sometimes in the singular and sometimes in the plural, and it is usually more convenient to avoid having separate headings. In this case it is up to the indexer to choose whether he will use the singular or the plural form; he must adhere consistently to his choice throughout the index. With a generalized type of noun, usually the plural is chosen.

The choice, however, can be left, as it were, to the index-user by adopting a kind of dual-purpose keyword: "Tree(s)"; "Index(es)"; "Entry(-ies)". This method is frequently employed. But some words have a quite different sense in the plural, and then separate headings are essential. Such a word is "damage", which means merely harm or injury, whereas the word "damages" denotes a legally awarded compensation for some loss or injury.

Here is an example of an entry with a combined singular and plural heading:

Index(es):
    analytical, 3.3
    basic requirements for an, 6.1
    definition of an, 2.1
    types or kinds of, 3
    user of, *see* User of the index

Particularization of headings

To what extent headings can be expanded will depend, of course, on the total amount of space allowed for the index, as well as on the type of work that is being indexed. For example, for the index to a very light-weight book of reminiscences a mere list of proper names with their appropriate references may possibly prove adequate. But, in general, a simple heading (i.e. keyword alone) plus reference(s) rarely makes a satisfactory entry. Thus, "Oxford-shire, 125–7", alone and unadorned, provides not a clue to the *raison d'être* of the county's mention in the text. But "Oxfordshire, an outing in" does pin-point the allusion and indicates at once to the user whether it is the item he is seeking. In nearly every heading, then, some kind of modification and/or qualification will be needed. (If it can be so contrived that the elaborated heading will fit one printed line of a double-column index, so much the better.)

Perhaps I may be allowed to illustrate this principle by an example in my own experience. *Winston S. Churchill*, Vol. 1: *Youth*, by the late Hon. Randolph S. Churchill (1966), related how Winston, when he was at his preparatory school, twice wrote to his mother expressing a desire to see "Buffalo Bill". It could have been entered in the index as: "Buffalo Bill, 90". But that seemed to lack point, so my entry ran:

> Buffalo Bill (W. F. Cody, 1845–1917), WSC
>   wants to see (1887), 90 *bis*

It so happened that in a press notice of the book this particular entry was singled out for praise. The whole thing (less the reference at the end) constitutes the heading; "Buffalo" is the keyword, "(W. F. Cody, 1845–1917)" forms a qualification; and "WSC want to see (1887)" is a modification. The insertion of Cody's dates may be regarded as a trimming. It is certainly not an essential practice. In this case the author used to insist on dates being given for most of the characters in his biographies and, although this involves additional research on the part of the indexer, it can, I think, be helpful to the reader. The other date, timing the occurrence of the modification, is certainly useful and can be provided from the text. The use of *bis* after the reference number is explained on pp. 107–8. There was no subheading to this entry and no cross-reference was required from "Cody, W. F." as that name was not mentioned in the text.

As it stands, the "Buffalo Bill" entry plainly constitutes pretty full indexing and, with the majority of the other entries treated on a similar scale, the index will require a generous allowance of space, which in this instance was fortunately forthcoming. In a "literary" index (that is, as opposed to a scientific, technical or legal one) such elaborate headings add a certain attractiveness, and an index in narrative form can indeed become readable and in parts even exciting. At the same time, it must not be forgotten that the function of headings (and of subheadings) is to act as a pointer to some statement in the text – they must not usurp the province of a synopsis or a *précis*. For this reason and for the sake of economy the wording of modifications must be cut to the minimum needed to convey the sense (as in "WSC wants to see" above); nor need they slavishly follow the actual words used in the text. On the other hand, where the text cites a striking utterance by or about some great man, this can, if sufficiently succinct, be quoted verbatim in the heading or one of the subheadings under that man's name. Thus, to take as an example a sub-entry under the heading "Edward VII, King" in the index to Richard Hough's

First Sea Lord (1969), a biography of Admiral Lord Fisher of Kilverstone:

> "Admiral Sir John Fisher is to do no work on Sundays . . . By Command, Edward R", 190, 276

Such quotations are of the utmost utility to the reader and are especially welcomed by reviewers, who, as one of them has admitted, "are known sometimes to begin with a glance through the index" (and occasionally to neglect to read through the book in consequence). Should the quotation be of inordinate length, it may be abbreviated to something like this:

> q. [=quoted] on JF's Sunday hours at Admiralty

The heading, "Edward VII, King", brings us to the question of inverted headings.

Inverted headings

A compound heading (or subheading) is said to be inverted when the normal order of its elements is transposed, in order that the second (or a later) element may supply the keyword:

> Coins, copper
> Drug addiction, teen-age
> Shaw, George Bernard

As regards the first example, whether or not the heading ought to be inverted would depend on whom the text was designed to appeal to – a metallurgist or a numismatist. If "copper coins" referred to one section of a whole chapter or article devoted to the coinage, then the heading would have to be left uninverted. Similarly, if the whole book concerned drugs, the inversion of the second heading would be unnecessary.

The fewer the words whose natural order is upset by the inversion, the better. In the index to a book or periodical there is no place for a multi-transposition of the inventory type beloved by army quartermaster-sergeants, such as:

> Tents, bell, canvas, soldiers, for the use of

But what are we to make of the following heading to be found in the index to the much-consulted *British Surgical Practice*? –

Diet, anus, artificial, patients with, for[1]

This seems almost eligible for inclusion in the present work's final chapter!

The following are examples of the kinds of compound heading that usually require inversion.

1) Surnames, preceded by forenames or initials; also peerage titles:

George-Brown, Rt Hon. Lord
Smith, W. H., & Son Ltd
Salisbury, 3rd Marquess of
Canterbury, Archbishop of [but better under surname]

But the names of firms and companies sometimes present complications. "Smith, W. H., & Son Ltd", as above, will stand, and this is the form adopted (although entirely bereft of commas) in the London telephone directories which until 1975 could be regarded as, on the whole, models of good arrangement.[2]

It becomes more difficult to deal with a company designated (shall we say?) Ellis Charles & Co. Ltd, where "Ellis" is a Christian name. If we simply invert and list it as Charles, Ellis, & Co. Ltd, it might be ambiguous, since many people, ignoring the comma after "Ellis", might jump to the conclusion that Charles and Ellis were partners and would, therefore, address the company exactly as appearing in the index. Several years ago, when I was Hon. Secretary of the Society of Indexers, I was consulted by the

---

[1] Attention was drawn to this and other equally odd headings in the same index by Mr John L. Thornton, FLA, in a lecture on "Medical Indexing" in the Society of Indexers' Training Course. Most indexers would agree with his suggestion that the offending heading would have been far better left thus: "Diet for patients with artificial anus". But that is not a case of inversion at all, since the keyword remains unaltered.

[2] But I came across a curious lapse in alphabetical order in the L–R volume for 1969, where on page 2033 three Laurie headings were followed by:

Laurice of London
Lauricella Remo
Lauricks, W.A.

followed by dozens more of Laurie entries. It is surprising that Lauricella Remo was not entered at all under R among the other Remo entries.

proprietor of a well-known trade directory. He was baffled by the fact that British publishing houses employ three different ways of setting out trading names, and wondered which to use:

1) Wedgwood & Sons, Ltd, Josiah
2) Wedgwood, Josiah, & Sons Ltd
3) Wedgwood (Josiah) & Sons Ltd

1) Worcester Royal Porcelain Co. Ltd, The
2) Worcester, The, Royal Porcelain Co. Ltd
3) Worcester (The) Royal Porcelain Co. Ltd

My reply as regards the first series was (and is) that (1) is incorrect, since it is important that the forename shall immediately follow the surname, as determining the heading's alphabetical order where (as so often) there is more than one with the same surname. But (2) and (3) can both be correctly used, my preference being for (3) with "Josiah" in parentheses – in the same way "(Ellis)" would solve the Ellis Charles problem above. On the other hand, in the second series, at the risk of appearing inconsistent I stated that the only correct version is (1), my reason being that the definite article is quite unimportant and could even be omitted altogether (but not in "*Times, The*").

The Board of Trade's *Register of Companies and Limited Partnerships,* while it confirms my suggested order for The Worcester Royal Porcelain Co., indexes Josiah Wedgwood & Sons under J. This is because there, apart from the inversion of the initial definite article, every company's name is entered exactly as originally registered. This procedure has increasingly come into favour among indexers in recent years, and indeed the new British Standard (BS 3700: 1976, para. 5.2.2.7) recommends that names of "corporate bodies" (i.e. colleges etc. as well as business names) should "normally" be indexed without transposition. This is currently a bone of contention among indexers. I would recommend that in certain cases, as for example the ladies' fashion store, Peter Robinson, where the Christian name is an integral part of the trade name, the heading need not be inverted.[1] But then a double entry is desirable (one entry being, if necessary, merely a cross-reference).

[1] The *Anglo-American Cataloguing Rules 1967* provide for the name to be inverted only if it begins with initials or an abbreviated forename. Thus we would have "Peter Robinson", but "Robinson (P.) & Co.", or "Jones (Wm.) Ltd".

I suggest, therefore, that the safest way of inverting names of firms and companies is as follows:

Allen (George) & Unwin Ltd
Charles (Ellis) & Son Ltd
Peter Robinson
Robinson, Peter, *see* Peter Robinson
Smith (W. H.) & Sons Ltd
Wedgwood (Josiah) & Sons Ltd
Worcester Royal Porcelain Co. Ltd, The

2) Names of individual saints, popes, monarchs and certain other dignitaries:

George, Saint
Thomas More, Saint, *see* More, Sir Thomas
Paul VI, Pope
Napoleon III, Emperor
John, Don, of Austria
   or, if it is preferred, John of Austria, Don
Ferdinand, Archduke

But it should be noted that saints' days are not inverted, nor are the names of institutions called after any individual in one of the above classes:

St George's Day
St Bartholomew's Hospital
King George's Fund for Sailors

3) Certain geographical names, often representing non-political partitions:

England, Eastern [but East Anglia, Great Britain, North Britain should be left uninverted]
Manchester, East; Bristol, North; Barnet, High [but New Barnet; High Wycombe; West Ham. The dividing line here is thinly drawn.]
Korea, North; Vietnam, South. [Both are usually so indexed, but long-established separate entities, such as states and provinces, are not to be inverted: North Carolina; South Carolina; Western Australia.]
Biscay, Bay of; Panama, Isthmus of; Good Hope, Cape of [but the *Oxford Atlas* indexes this also under Cape of Good Hope and this form might be handy where the text refers to "The Cape", unless the allusion is to Cape Province or the old Cape Colony]

4) The definite and indefinite articles:

Ideal Husband, An
Royal Engineers, The

(Headings starting with the definite or indefinite article have already been dealt with, p. 43.)

5) Government departments:

Defence, Ministry of
Education & Science, Department of
Trade, Board of

As government departments are often indexed without inversion, it may be as well to provide a cross-reference from the uninverted form. This can sometimes be done in the following shortened form:

Boards, *see* Trade, Board of . . .
Ministries, *see* Agriculture; Defence . . .

Societies and institutions are normally indexed without inversion, other than as affecting the definite article:[1]

Institute of Inventors, the
Society of Indexers, the

But Robert L. Collison, in the indexes to some of his books, gives a double entry (under I as well as S) for the Society of Indexers, as does also the London telephone directory (under A and S) for the Society of Authors, but not for the Institute of Inventors, which is entered under the first proper name alone.

A double entry (i.e. of the uninverted as well as the inverted form) is sometimes convenient in certain instances of classes (3) and (5) of inverted headings above. Double entries in connexion with references and cross-references will be discussed in Chapter 6.

---

[1] Foreign institutions are usually indexed in British publications either under their indigenous title or else preceded by the name of the country:

l'Institut français [under I]
United States [or US] Department of Commerce

Unnecessary headings

In selecting our headings we are likely to alight particularly upon the proper names in the text, and probably nine times out of ten a proper name will provide a fitting entry. But we must beware of so using each such name indiscriminately and without regard to its importance in the author's scheme. Thus, if the text tells us that a certain character travelled to Dover via Folkestone, then a heading for Folkestone, on the strength of this allusion alone and unless a subsequent passage attaches some special significance to his having broken his journey there, will be quite useless and will merely clutter up the index. Or again, a mere comparison such as "Harold Wilson, like some modern Robin Hood . . ." does not call for an entry under Hood, Robin.

This shows how useful it is to be able (whenever possible) to read through the complete text before embarking on the index, and thus to acquire a prior sense of perspective of the whole structure.

A number of further instances of unnecessary (because hopelessly futile) headings are listed by Wheatley in his *How to Make an Index*. Here, *pour rire*, are a few:

Eastern Desert on Foot, Through an
Foot, Through an Eastern Desert on
Through an Eastern Desert on Foot

Foot in it, On Putting One's
On Putting One's Foot in it

The last pair aptly describes what the indexer has succeeded in doing. These examples were extracted from actual indexes to periodicals and the headings had obviously been obtained by ringing the changes on the wording of some article's *title* instead of indexing the *subject* of the article. This will be discussed below, in Chapter 8. It applies also to the indexing of chapter headings in a book.

No headings are required for any matter in a book's title page, dedication, table of contents or synopses at the head of chapters. Otherwise all matter should be well covered, including appendixes – though glossaries and bibliographies only rarely need to be indexed.

Another form of unnecessary heading in a book index may be

provided by the subject of the book itself. Thus, in the index to a book devoted wholly to the theme of France, one should not expect to find that word used as a heading, unless possibly as "France, Anatole", or "France, Banque de", although the latter would be better if entered as "Banque de France".

In 1961 the late Gordon Carey read to the Society of Indexers a thought-provoking paper which he called "No Room at the Top".[1] In this he claimed that the above principle could sometimes be extended even to the subject of a biography, thus running counter to all established practice. But he had proved his point in his more than adequate index to *The Memoirs of Lord Ismay* (1960), which contains no entry for that nobleman's name. That, however, is an autobiography and the author did not expatiate on his own personality. In a previous index to *Haldane of Cloan*, by Dudley Sommer (1960), the repeated emphasis in the text on certain of Haldane's personal traits, as also the fact that some events of his career had no obvious keyword of their own, had forced Carey to compromise to the extent of furnishing a brief entry under "Haldane, Richard Burdon", consisting of about a dozen of the main events of his career and of his *Personal traits,* the latter being listed in alphabetical order.

Compare this with the American indexes to the well-known Boswell series, where under Boswell, James, we are given entries stretching to up to $5\frac{1}{2}$ pages (or eleven columns). (In the personal entry in the index to *Boswell in Search of a Wife* (1957), it is not pretty to find as many as 38 allusions to Boswell's catching, escaping from, or being treated for, the pox. I suggest that these had better been relegated to a separate heading under the word "pox".) With all this haystack piled up around the index-user's needles, he almost needs an auxiliary index to find the object of his search!

We must certainly, therefore, when compiling the index to a biography, beware of overloading the entry for its central figure. This brings us to the topic of subheadings.

Subheadings

Subheadings help to widen the context of a heading. Entries with only a very few page references may not need any subheadings.

[1] *The Indexer*, Vol. 2, No. 4 (Autumn 1961), pp. 120–3.

But even when there are only two references, it may be necessary to supply a subheading for each, if both are important and deal with different aspects of the main heading.

Subheadings are the vassals of their headings and should always (like ordinary modifications) have a close connexion with their lords and masters. They should not be in that position at all, except perhaps by way of having a cross-reference from them, if worthy to be promoted to an independent status as headings in their own right. Where a heading comprises the whole subject matter of a complete chapter or periodical article or section of either, then it is unnecessary and constitutes bad indexing (as involving a waste of space as well as savouring of classification – see pp. 96–100) to use as subheadings all its subsections. In such a case they should be given separate headings, and the main entry's subheadings should be confined to outside allusions to the topic in the text; these should be given the main entry's reference number only when alluded to in the main section as well. Thus:

Not

Indexes, 399–430
  alphabetizing, 414–20, 421
  author-title, 429, 444
  column width in, 423, 444
  cross-references in, 402–3
  defined, 400–3
  editing, 51
  editing cards for, 420–2
  first page number of, 81
  form of, examples, 428–9
  indexes vs. *indices*, 129
  justified lines in, 424, 440
        etc.

but

Indexes, 399–430
  author-title, 429, 444
  column width in, 423, 444
  editing, 51, 420–2
  first page number of, 81
  indexes vs. *indices*, 129
  justified lines in, 424–440
        etc.

It should be observed how much shorter is the second version (which I suggest is the more correct), and how much space would have been saved by the adoption of a similar method in an index where numerous entries are treated in the manner of the first. In fairness, however, it must be pointed out that the actual index[1] from which the above example on the left is cited – with page references substituted for the paragraph references of the original – does not in fact give the group reference (399–430) for the heading,

[1] From *A Manual of Style*, 12th edition (University of Chicago Press, 1969).

although many of the subheadings could have been eliminated had it done so; also that it *does* provide separate headings for all the subheadings whose references are covered by that group reference.

There are two distinct ways of setting out subheadings, and according to which method is chosen will depend their treatment. They may be arranged in columnar or line-by-line form, or else they may be "run-on". The latter method makes up in economy of space what it lacks in the clarity and ease of reference inherent in the line-by-line system (sometimes referred to as the "indented" style).

Thebes, city of (Egypt), 123
  area around, 23–41
  art of, 151
  Assyrians sack, 24
  Horemheb's destructiveness
    in, 209–10
  map of tombs in, *43*
  palaces in, 86
  priesthood of, 85
  temple of Mut in, 36
  Tutankhamen's birth in,
    103
  West, royal cache at, *39*
  workshops on west bank
    of, 161

Thebes, city of (Egypt), 123; area around, 23–41; art of, 151; Assyrians sack, 24; Horemheb's destructiveness in, 209–10; map of tombs in, *43*; palaces in, 86; priesthood of, 85; temple of Mut in, 36; Tutankhamen's birth in, 103; West, royal cache at, *39*; workshops on west bank of, 161

The difference between the two methods is obvious at a glance. The line-by-line setting has the more attractive appearance and renders it far easier to find what one is seeking. On the other hand, it occupies much more space than the other.

Where this system is used, the subheadings should be arranged in strictly alphabetical order of keywords, although a few indexers try to save themselves trouble by keeping them in the reference order of the pages (or paragraphs) in which the items first occur. There are, however, one or two exceptional cases in which an entry may have its subheadings more conveniently in numerical or chronological order:

French governments
  Second Republic
  Third Republic
  Fourth Republic

Society of Indexers, The
  Third Annual Report
  Fourth Annual Report
  Fifth Annual Report

Dynasties, Chinese
  Shang (1766–1112 BC)
  Han (206 BC–AD 186)
  Ming (1318–1644)

One advantage of the line-by-line method is that it allows for sub-subheadings, so frequently encountered in scientific and technological indexing. Except, however, in legal indexes, it is unsafe to subdivide further than sub-subheadings. Indeed, many indexers of straight "literary" works prefer not to use sub-subheadings, as savouring of systematic classification; they can be quite easily avoided by the simple expedient of converting the subheading concerned into a cross-reference to a separate heading of its own, under which can be given as subheadings what would have been sub-subheadings in the main entry. Thus, to amplify the instance already referred to earlier in this chapter:

Not
  Cross-references
    definition of, 2.5
    "see", 2.2; 4.4
      definition of, 2.5
      inverted forms and, 4.4
      punctuation for, 6.1
    synonyms referred to through,
      4.2

but
  Cross-references
    definition of, 2.5
    "see", *see* "See" cross-references
    synonyms referred to through,
      4.2
  "See" cross-references, 2.2; 4.4
    definition of, 2.5
    inverted forms and, 4.4
    punctuation for, 6.1

It will be noticed that in every case in the above examples the subheading in sense *precedes* the main heading, and this is the commonest form. But very frequently subheadings in sense *follow* the heading, and Carey, in his valuable pamphlet, *Making an Index* (3rd edn, 1963), suggests that the two classes should not be mixed under the same heading. Thus, we can have:

Growth, point of minimum
Growth, of aquatic animals
  of bone
  of horns,
    etc.

Here, however, the second heading could have been avoided by the simple device of putting all the modifications in the possessive case ("aquatic animals' "; "bone's", etc.). But it is frequently found more convenient not to separate the two classes, especially in a long entry:

Letters
   and legends
   as musical notes
   names of
   for rhyme schemes
   superior, in classical references
                etc.

In all such instances, the conjunctions "and" and "as" and the prepositions "for", "in", "of", "to", with which the subheading may start, must be ignored in determining its alphabetical order, just as shown.

Whether subheadings are in line-by-line order or are run-on, they must clearly have a logical relationship to the main heading. In a well-constituted index they should also bear a close grammatical relationship. In other words, it should be possible to make good grammatical sense by joining heading and subheading in the normal order of the combined phrase. Hence the "of", "and", "for" and "through" at the end of the subheadings in the "Cross-references" example above. Some indexers look upon these particles as ungainly knobs and excrescences, to be hacked off. In doing so, they may plead they are saving space; but the result is often ambiguity.

Run-on subheadings can be set either in alphabetical order, as in the "Thebes" example above, or in chronological order. Whichever method is chosen should be adhered to consistently throughout any one index, except that in a chronological-order index that order may not lend itself to one or two entries; an instance would be the "characteristics" of the hero-subject of a biography, and here the various subheadings (or sub-subheadings) – Affability, Bibulousness, etc., etc. – would be preferably arranged in alphabetical order.

Where the subheadings are arranged alphabetically, whether they be in line-by-line or run-on form, the keyword must be chosen with almost as much care as for headings. I say "almost as much care", because even the longest entry will obviously include far fewer subheadings than the whole index has headings, so that in the former case it will be that much easier to find an ineptly chosen keyword.

Chronological subheadings are mainly confined to the indexes to histories and biographies. Their order in the index must be kept strictly chronological, irrespective of the page-reference order in the text. Some while ago I was indexing a memoir in which the biographee's funeral is described as early as page 12, in an account of the ancestral estate. This was indexed, therefore, as the very last of the subheadings under the name of the estate. (It was not put under the name of the biographee, for reasons given earlier.)

It has always, so far as I can discover, been customary to run on literally the whole of any set of subheadings, even when they extend to several columns. This seemed to me not only to produce a distasteful appearance but also (and more importantly) to be wholly inimical to any ease of reference whatever. I therefore take any credit that may be due for having devised the splitting up of any long list of subheadings into paragraphs. Readers are invited to compare the two systems, as shown in the examples below. It is believed that they will agree that, while not very much longer than the other, that on the right has a more pleasing aspect and is far the more readable:

Admiralty, Board of
  sends JF special letter of thanks (1864), 49–50: JF hoped for a London appointment from (1870), 53; depended on War Office for stores, 54, 86–8; intervenes to secure what JF wants for *Inflexible*, 65; had declined to make Prince Albert an Admiral of the Fleet, 66; message of sympathy to JF during dysentery, 74; inter-departmental committee with War Office, 88; JF a member of (1892), 92; orders JF's flag hoisted as C-in-C, Mediterranean (1899), 116–17; JF's attack on (1899–1902), 120, 127–33, 139; JF 2nd Naval Lord (1902), 139, 146–59; and the Imperial Defence Committee, 165; practi-

Admiralty, Board of
  sends JF special letter of thanks (1864), 49–50; JF hoped for a London appointment from (1870), 53; depended on War Office for stores, 54, 86–8; intervenes to secure what JF wants for *Inflexible*, 65; had declined to make Prince Albert an Admiral of the Fleet, 66; message of sympathy to JF during dysentery, 74; inter-departmental committee with War Office, 88

  JF a member of (1892), 92; orders JF's flag hoisted as C-in-C, Mediterranean (1899), 116–17; JF's attack on (1899–1902), 120, 127–33, 139; JF 2nd Naval Lord (1902), 139, 146–59; and the Imperial Defence Committee, 165;

cally run by JF (from Portsmouth), Battenberg and Tyrwhitt (1904), 174; JF 1st Sea Lord (1904), 178; at his desk at 6 a.m. at latest, 189; his day's work at, 189–90; Committee on Designs (1904), *see* Committee on; Committees on Two-power Standard (1905), 253; issues memorandum on redeployment (1906), 202; "always knows better than the Foreign Office" – JF to the King (1906), 205; Beresford's attacks on, 209, 215–17, 218–35, 360–2; JF's memo. to, on Beresford (1907), 219; Beresford's confrontation with, 219–20, 360–2; orders withdrawal of LCB's memo. on Bridgeman, 221; "will have to recognize" role of CID, 275; riles LCB by refusing to dismiss Scott, 223; Inquiry into its administration, 224–5 (*see also* Asquith Committee); JF and all the, threaten to resign (1908 and 1909), 261, 288

practically run by JF (from Portsmouth), Battenberg and Tyrwhitt (1904), 174

JF 1st Sea Lord (1904), 178; at his desk at 6 a.m. at latest, 189; his day's work at, 189–90; Committee on Designs (1904), *see* Committee on; Committees on Two-power Standard (1905), 253; issues memorandum on redeployment (1906), 202; "always knows better than the Foreign Office" – JF to the King (1906), 205

Beresford's attacks on, 209, 215–17, 218–35, 360–2; JF's memo. to, on Beresford (1907), 219; Beresford's confrontation with, 219–20, 360–2; orders withdrawal of LCB's memo. on Bridgeman, 221; "will have to recognize" role of CID, 275; riles LCB by refusing to dismiss Scott, 223; Inquiry into its administration, 224–5 (*see also* Asquith Committee); JF and all the, threaten to resign (1908 and 1909), 261, 288

Readers who may wish to use the second system are advised to start a new paragraph after about every sixth subheading. They should contrive, if possible, to ensure that each paragraph opens with a subheading of some significance. If the subheadings are arranged alphabetically, it may be neat and convenient to begin each letter of the alphabet with a new paragraph.

Punctuation of headings and subheadings

Comma. It used to be regarded as essential to insert a comma at the end of each heading and subheading before the first page (or paragraph) reference, or a "see" cross-reference. But it is now allowable to dispense with that comma and substitute an extra space. This was provided for in the British Standard on the preparation of indexes (BS 3700: 1964), so when I came to compile the index to that useful pamphlet, I decided to give the new system a trial. Unfortunately, my experiment ran into difficulty. In my instructions to the printer I had omitted to emphasize the need for that space, and the resulting entries on my proofs were somewhat disconcerting:

> Author of text
>   help from 4.1
>   index compiled by *foreword*
> Bold type, use of 6.2
> Books, indexing of *foreword* 1a
> Directives, italic type for 6.2

In consequence the whole of the ten-page index had to be reset, and I have ever since reverted to using that final comma.

A comma is always required between the two elements of an inverted heading or subheading. It has also a most important use in marking which part of a subheading connects with the heading:

> Admiralty, Board of
>   JF's memo to, on Beresford (1907)
>   JF and all the, threaten to resign (1908)
>   "everything was wrong" at, on JF's return (1914)

Otherwise, in both headings and subheadings, the comma enjoys its normal function of appropriately dividing a sentence or phrase.

Colon. The colon has one special, highly important role in connexion with an entry that has run-on subheadings, but no references immediately following the heading. If the first subheading is made to start on the next line *below* the heading, all is well, for the indention obviates the necessity of any punctuation after the heading. (See the "Admiralty, Board of" example above.) But frequently, to save space, the first subheading is made to start on the same line as the heading. Now if a comma is placed after the heading, as is far too often done, then the first subheading must strictly be regarded as a mere qualification of that heading, and all the subsequent subheadings would have to apply to both. This will be made clearer by the following example:

> Cathedrals: Australian, 644; plans of, 410–3; Early Christian, 262 . . .

As it stands, this all makes good sense. But just substitute a comma for the colon ("Cathedrals, Australian . . .") and all the later subheadings become associated with Australian cathedrals, so that we are presented with the astonishing phenomenon of an Early Christian cathedral in the Antipodes.

A similar necessity for a colon applies also to a line-by-line entry if, in the absence of any references after the heading, the first sub-entry is allowed to begin on the top line.

Semicolon. A semicolon is the normal punctuation employed to separate one sub-entry from the next in a run-on entry. In a line-by-line entry the sub-entries are separated naturally. (See the "Admiralty, Board of" example, above.)

Full stop. The full stop, so frequently occurring in the text, has no use in the index, except (a) to mark an abbreviation, such as "Rev." or "R.A.F."; (b) before "See also", where that cross-reference is placed at the end of an entry or sub-entry. (But see below, p. 112.)

Question mark. Besides its ordinary use at the end of a quoted question (e.g. under *Macbeth*: "Can such things be?"), the mark of interrogation can sometimes be used with effect to show very briefly that the topic of the heading or subheading has been debated as a matter of controversy in the text:

Bacon or Shakespeare?
Grammar Schools or Comprehensives?
Henry VII, Princes in the Tower murdered by?

Exclamation mark. This should be used very sparingly in an index (apart from coming after some exclamation quoted from the text). The mark can, however, be employed occasionally to indicate the author's surprise or disapproval. Two instances occur in successive entries in the index to Richard Hough's *First Sea Lord*:

George V, King
   his victory speech (1918) – JF's name omitted!, 346
German Fleet in World War I
   surrender of (1918) – JF not invited to ceremony!, 356

The indexer's "neutrality"?

In selecting and modifying his headings and subheadings the indexer must be careful always to reflect the views of his author.

His, alas, is not properly a creative task and he must resist the temptation to inject his own opinions, political or otherwise. That there is a real danger of this happening is shown by the cry of Lord Macaulay in a letter to his publishers: "Let no damned Tory make the index to my History".

If the author of the text has taken a decided line, one way or the other, then the indexer must do likewise. This sometimes results in unjustified criticism. Thus, in his *Asquith* (1964) Roy Jenkins denounced the entry under "Maurice, Major-General Sir Frederick", in Lloyd George's memoirs, as being highly tendentious. An index, he declared, ought to be "neutral". But how, it may be asked, can the index be more neutral than the text upon which it is based?

An even more flagrantly polemical example is to be found in the index to the American *Accessories after the Fact*, by Sylvia Meagher (1967), dealing with the assassination of President Kennedy. Commenting on this index in *Book World*, George Cook says:

> Under "Warren Commission" we find a total of 422 page references under the following subheadings: "bias and predisposition"; "delays in investigation of evidence"; "failure to investigate suspicious circumstances"; "illogical and double standard"; "impeachment of witnesses"; "inadequate and incomplete investigation"; "inattention or indifference to evidence"; "manipulation and distorted presentation of facts".

But this index was compiled by the authoress of *Accessories* herself, so it can scarcely have misrepresented her views. In the matters complained of, at any rate, therefore, the indexes to both the above books must be regarded as impeccable.

A previous book by Mrs Meagher was, however, more susceptible to inculpation. This was her *Subject Guide to the Warren Report*, which was *all* index from cover to cover. In this she invented the brilliant "negative reference" to subjects which did *not* appear in the Report but which she thought should have been included. Such a practice is normally no part of an indexer's task.

CHAPTER FOUR
Proper Name Headings

Have very few heads, except proper names. . . . The best rule is to keep close to proper names, and never to deviate from that rule without some special occasion.

Thomas Babington Macaulay (1800–1859),
advice to the indexer of his *History of England* (1848–1855)

Lord Macaulay had himself been an indexer, and it was no doubt his experience of having compiled, at the age of fifteen, the index to the thirteenth volume of the *Christian Observer* that prompted him to tender the above piece of advice. It is, however, too sweeping, and the original edition of his *History* would have been better served by a fuller index containing analysis of more of the subject matter of that remarkable work. Again, Macaulay was only speaking of historical indexing, while there are many topics (e.g. philosophy and technology) that demand a considerable predominance of subject entries.

None the less, as already indicated, the great majority of proper names in the text will form indexable headings. Their indexing is usually straightforward enough, although here, as elsewhere, there are a few basic rules to be generally observed and, as we shall see later, some problems present themselves in connexion with certain foreign names.

PERSONAL NAMES

A place in the index should be reserved for nearly every person's name occurring in the text. A name, however, that is only mentioned in a reference note or a bibliography is usually omitted. But in both cases such names may require indexing in medical and scientific works. Another exception might have to be made in the case of a list of say twenty or thirty people (nowhere else mentioned in the text) who happened to be present on some notable occasion. If they were not particularly prominent persons and if nothing else was said about them beyond their presence at the function, then surely to include their names in the index would be to overload it. Consider, too, the following passage from Kenneth Rose's *Superior Person* (1969):

> He therefore abandoned himself to books, consuming two at a time. In this way he sampled Milton, Macaulay, Stevenson, Goethe, Voltaire, Thackeray, Carlyle, George Eliot, Cervantes, Froude and Disraeli.

Of this list of authors, the only name that is thought to deserve inclusion in the index is Disraeli, who also has other more substantial allusions elsewhere in the book. The whole passage is indexed simply as a sub-subheading, "reading", under the personal entry of Curzon, George Nathaniel, the subheading being "pastimes".

Form of heading

Where the author gives the forename (or initials) of a character, then the name should appear in the index in exactly the same form as in the text. Thus, Eliot, T. S., *not* Eliot, Thomas Stearns. But in a book devoted entirely or mainly to the poet his personal entry would have to quote the name in full. Similarly, Cervantes should only be indexed as Cervantes Saavedra, Miguel de, if the author insists on presenting him to us as Cervantes Saavedra; otherwise Cervantes, Miguel de, will suffice.

When in different parts of the text the same person's name appears in more than one form, as for instance, Wilfrid Blunt, W. S. Blunt and Wilfrid Scawen Blunt, then the indexer should choose the most complete form: Blunt, Wilfrid Scawen. Or again, Cervantes Saavedra, Miguel de.

Sometimes it happens that an author will give only the surname of someone (probably a writer well known in the context). In such a case it behoves the indexer to bestir himself to ascertain the forename or initials, because nothing looks untidier than an index that contains some of its surname headings standing alone and unadorned ("Blunt, 297"); moreover it can be the cause of confusion, as where there is more than one person with the same surname. The quest may need some little ingenuity. Perhaps the name concerned will be found in full in the bibliography, if the book being indexed has one. Otherwise, if he has access to the author, the indexer can approach him. Or the name may be found in the index to a work on a similar subject, or in an encyclopaedia, or the catalogue of the British Library, or an international dictionary of biography.

Thus, if we were compiling an index to the indexless *Alphabetical Subject Indication of Information*, by John Metcalfe (1965), we should come across on page 27 the following sentence:

> Cutter notes that Poole's arrangement of his entries was the same as Crestadoro's.

Here there are three surnames unaccompanied by forenames or initials. It might not be easy for the indexer to consult the author, for he lives in New South Wales, at the other side of the world. But by referring to the index of another book by the same author, *Information Indexing* (1957), we can readily fill in the blanks:

Crestadoro, A.
Cutter, C. A.
Poole, William Frederick

It may be that a narrative contains a lively account of the sayings or doings of some minor character, whose name thus becomes indexable. If only one element is provided in the text and because of his obscurity, or for some other reason, it would be practically impossible to trace any fuller name, then sufficient description must be added in parentheses to facilitate identification:

Beaumont, Mr (Shakespearean lecturer)
"Chloe" (WSC's dog)
Edney (Lord Randolph's butler)
Johnny (cabin boy in SS *Aurora*)

The use of *Mr* after Beaumont in the above examples is exceptional. For untitled persons their forenames suffice (or, if those are lacking in the text, then the initials) as a qualification of the surname keyword. Heed should be paid to Dr Johnson's angry outburst, as

related by Boswell, when a certain Mr Flaxman was mentioned in
his company:

> Let me hear no more of him, Sir. That is the fellow who made the index
> to my *Ramblers*, and set down the name of Milton thus: Milton, *Mr.* John.[1]

Honorifics, however, marking military, academic or theological
distinctions, if preceding the name (e.g. Sgt., Col., Dr, Rev., Prof.)
should be inserted in the index entry, and it is often advisable to
use Mrs in the case of a married woman:

Balfour, Arthur James
Eddy, Mrs Mary Baker
Mitchell, Lieut-Col. Colin
Rowse, Dr A. L.
Temple, Most Rev. Frederick
Ward, Mrs Humphry[2]

The names of clergy, like those of knights or baronets, should
always include a Christian name – Smith, Rev. Alfred, not Smith,
Rev. A., and certainly not Smith, Rev.

The indexer must follow the usage of the text, although if he
discovers any striking inaccuracies or discrepancies of spelling or
statement in the uncorrected page proofs from which he is working, then it is open to him to advise the author or publisher's
editor accordingly. But if the text is spelt in American fashion, he
must not try to translate his index into English. Nor must he, if
throughout the text the great discoverer is called by his Spanish
name, Cristobal Colon, or by his actual Genoese name, Cristofor
Colombo, use for the principal index entry the more familiar
variant, Columbus, Christopher; a cross-reference from the last
name would, however, be virtually essential.

Pseudonyms

Pseudonyms consist usually of authors' pen names, or names that
have been assumed for some such purpose as to enlist in the
Foreign Legion, or to court obscurity after disgrace, as Oscar
Wilde ended his days in Paris under the name of Sebastian

[1] This first index to *The Rambler* (Flaxman's, 1752) contained six references under
Milton, Mr. John.
[2] There must be a cross-reference from Ward, Mary Augusta, the actual name of
the novelist, if she is also alluded to thus in the text.

Melmoth. If the real name is not mentioned in the text, there is no need to give it a separate entry in the index.

The pseudonym in an index heading, however, should be immediately followed by the real name in parentheses; this is not in order to display the indexer's erudition, but to avoid confusion of authorship:

> "Eliot, George" (Mary Ann Evans)
> "Ouida" (Marie Louise de la Ramée)
> "Ross, Martin"[1] (Violet Florence Martine)

Where both pseudonym(s) and real name are referred to in the text, the latter should form the principal entry, with cross-reference(s) from the former, as follows:

> Bell, Currer, *see* Brontë, Charlotte
> Brontë, Charlotte (pseudonym: Currer Bell)
>
> Creasey John[2] (pseudonyms: Michael Halliday; Kyle Hunt)
> Halliday Michael, *see* Creasey, John
> Hunt, Kyle, *see* Creasey, John
>
> Melmoth, Sebastian, *see* Wilde, Oscar
> Wilde, Oscar (pseudonym: Sebastian Melmoth)

Similar rules to those in the last three paragraphs apply to cases of a change of name. Examples are: the Duke of Windsor, who had been both Wales, Edward, Prince of, and Edward VIII, King of Great Britain and Northern Ireland; John Buchan, who late in life was created the 1st Baron Tweedsmuir; and Michael Sadler, who changed his surname to the older form of Sadleir.

The important thing in every case of a pseudonym or a changed name is to ensure that all statements in the text regarding either or any of the names shall be gathered together in one entry, and thus avoid committing the indexing offence of "scattered information" (see p. 92).

Repeated surnames

Where several persons with the same surname appear in the text, each should be carefully differentiated and identified and should be

---

[1] Of the famous Somerville and Ross collaboration in Irish novels.
[2] John Creasey uses four other pseudonyms, from Gordon Ashe to Jeremy York. A Californian novelist, Lauran Paine, writes under seventy-one!

given his or her own separate heading. This is not an appropriate occasion for the use of the much overworked "rule", or 3-em dash (———).

Thus, in the index to *The Life of the Right Reverend Ronald Knox*, by the late Evelyn Waugh (1959), no fewer than twenty-one members of the Knox family are named, the first few being listed as follows:

> Knox, Alexander (*RK's great-great-grandfather*)
> Knox, Alexander (*RK's great-uncle*)
> Knox, Dillwyn (*RK's brother*)
> Knox, Edmund Arbuthnott, Bishop of Manchester, 1903–21 (*RK's father*)
> Knox, Edmund Valpy ("Evoe") (*RK's brother*)
> Knox, Ellen (*RK's aunt*)
> Knox, Ellen Penelope (*RK's mother*)
> Knox, Emily (*RK's aunt*)
> Knox, Ethel (*RK's sister*)
> Knox, Ethel (*RK's stepmother*)
> Knox, Frances (*RK's grandmother*)

More than one of the above pairs of headings (e.g. Knox, Ethel) form, if divested of their qualifications in parentheses, good examples of *homonyms* – inverted compound homonyms. (For an explanation of homonyms and the order in which they should be indexed, see Chapter 7.)

Compound surnames

These may contain one or more hyphens (Douglas-Home; Plunkett-Ernle-Erle-Drax) or they may be unhyphened. The former present no difficulty; they should invariably be indexed under the initial letter of the first element of the hyphened name, although a cross-reference from the second element may occasionally be necessary where, for instance, the hyphen is first assumed in the course of the text's narrative. I say "invariably" despite a confident assertion in the Chicago *Manual of Style* (12th edn, 1969) that "Bannerman, Henry Campbell-" is the established usage. This is not borne out in the indexes to *Hansard* at the end of last century, which firmly place *Sir* Henry under C (with no cross-reference from B); and so with the encyclopaedias and other sources that I have consulted.

Exceptionally, and (to my way of thinking) rather eccentrically,

Who's Who has the following entry for the family name of the Dukes of Portland:

Cavendish-Bentinck, *see* Bentinck

Indexers are advised not to follow this example, the explanation of which is probably that the 1st Earl of Portland (in the present creation) was Hans William *Bentinck* (William of Orange's bosom friend) and it was the 3rd Duke who, after marrying the daughter of the Duke of Devonshire in 1801, assumed by royal licence the latter's surname (Cavendish) in addition to his own. Other hyphened surnames (including Plunkett-Ernle-Erle-Drax) are arranged in *Who's Who* in their normal alphabetical order.

The unhyphened compounds are not so easy to determine. Sir Winston Spencer Churchill, Andrew Bonar Law and David Lloyd George (who became Earl Lloyd-George of Dwyfor less than three months before his death in 1945), are three cases in point. It may not be generally known that Sir Winston's last two names had always been more accurately hyphened, and up to the end of 1951 the ever-punctilious *Court Circular* invariably referred to him as Spencer-Churchill; indeed *Debrett's Peerage, Baronetage, Knightage and Companionage* did so to the end of his life. But he himself has related how greatly he detested his coming in consequence at the end of the alphabetical roll-call at Harrow, and he always signed his name, "Winston S. Churchill". So it would be madness to flout the vast majority of index-users (who think of him only as "Churchill") by entering his name under "S", although a cross-reference from Spencer-Churchill is admissible and may even be advisable.

The case of Bonar Law is more difficult. It looks like a compound name, but in fact is not, and is correctly indexed as Law, Andrew Bonar, with a cross-reference from Bonar Law. Throughout his parliamentary career (1900–23) his name appeared in the index to *Hansard* under L (but with no cross-reference from under B). On the other hand, Robert Blake in his index to his standard life, *The Unknown Prime Minister* (1955), listed his hero under B. When I tackled him on this point, he justified his practice by saying that his readers would instinctively look for the name under that letter. It would have been quite permissible if only he had supplied a cross-reference from Law.

Lloyd George (hyphened since 1945) should always be indexed under L, and nowadays no cross-reference is necessary. But the indexers to *Hansard* played a curious trick. When the young politician entered Parliament in 1890, his name was entered as "Lloyd George, David", with no cross-reference from "George". But in 1911 for some reason he became "George, the Rt Hon. David Lloyd", and it was not until 1935 that any cross-reference from "Lloyd George" appeared.

Where the text fails to mention the forenames or initials of a character with a compound name – for instance, "The composer Vaughan Williams and the actor-manager Granville-Barker . . ." – it is the indexer's job – as mentioned earlier in this chapter – to supply these in the index:

> Granville-Barker, Harley
> Vaughan Williams, Ralph
> Williams, Ralph Vaughan, *see* Vaughan Williams

Where the indexer cannot readily determine whether a name is in fact a compound one, the safest plan is to use the last element for the chief entry:

> Crawford, Francis Marion (novelist)
> Marion Crawford, *see* Crawford, Francis

In such a case, provided the index-user's likely preference is borne in mind, it does not matter particularly which element is chosen, so long as a cross-reference from the other is supplied.

Compound surnames with prefixes

In *British* (or anglicized) and *American* names the prefix forms the keyword for the entry. The same rule applies to *Afrikaans* and *Italian* (but not to mediaeval or early modern Italian) names; as also to *Rumanian* names (except when the prefix is a "de", which should be placed after the other elements of the compound heading):

> à Beckett, Gilbert Abbott[1]
> Ap Rhys Price, Gen. Sir Henry

[1] But for the Norman name, Becket, Thomas à; or Thomas à Becket, Saint.

Ben Alexander, Shmuel ["Ben" denotes "son of"]
D'Annunzio, Gabriele [x Annunzio, Gabriele d']¹
De La Mare, Walter
De Valera, Eamon [a Cuban name; x Valera, Eamon de]
De Wet, Gen. Christian (Boer leader)
Dos Passos, John Roderigo
Du Maurier, George
Im Thurn, Sir Everard
Medici, Lorenzo de'
Robbia, Luca della [x Della Robbia, Luca]
Van Dine, S. S. [US crime-story writer]
Van Dyck, Sir Anthony

The prefixes to surnames of *French*, *German*, *Netherlands*, *Portuguese*, *Scandinavian* and *Spanish* persons are, in general, inverted and do not form keywords. There is, however, an important exception. In French surnames, where the prefix is the definite article or a preposition contracted with it (Le, La, Du, Des), then it will form the word of entry. This applies also to the definite article as a prefix to a Spanish name. But in German and Netherlands names "von der" and "van den" are both inverted:

Fonseca, Manoel da
Gaulle, Gen. Charles de [x De Gaulle]
Gogh, Vincent van [x Van Gogh]
Hallstöm, Gunnar af
Humboldt, Karl Wilhelm von
La Fontaine, Jean de
Las Casas, Bartolomé de [x Casas]
Zur Linde, Otto [x Linde, Otto zur]

For foreign names without prefixes, see pp. 76–83.

Royalty and nobility

Kings, queens, emperors and other hereditary rulers should be entered under their official names (usually a forename). The name in the heading should always be qualified by the country over which he or she rules, or ruled. A familiar epithet can be cross-referred from, if prominently alluded to in the text, e.g. Charles the Bold, *see* Charles, Duke of Burgundy; Frederick the Great, *see* Frederick II, King of Prussia. Or it can be added in parentheses, e.g. Suleiman I ("the Magnificent"), Sultan of the Turks. Where

¹ x denotes "cross-reference from".

there has been more than one ruler of the same name in a state, each must be distinguished by a Roman numeral. It may sometimes be expedient to add dates in parentheses in order to avoid risk of confusion between sovereigns with the same number but of different states:

> Anne, Princess, daughter of Q. Elizabeth II
> Charles II ("the Bold"), King of France (823–77)
> Charles II, King of Great Britain & Ireland (1630–85)
> Charles II, King of Spain (1661–1700)
> Elizabeth, Queen (-Mother), consort of George VI of Great Britain
> Elizabeth I, Queen of England
> Elizabeth II, Queen of Great Britain & Northern Ireland
> Victor Emmanuel II, King of Italy
> Wales, Charles, Prince of (b.1948)

In most cases peers should be indexed under their titles (by which they are commonly known and which they invariably use for their signatures) rather than under their family names, which, however, if alluded to in the text, should be cross-referred from. Titles of nobility in this rule include courtesy titles, e.g. Cranborne, Viscount (eldest son of the Marquis of Salisbury). It should be noted, in passing, that the authorities are somewhat divided on this matter, since the *Dictionary of National Biography*, the *Dictionary of Universal Biography* (Hyamson) and the British Library catalogue all list noblemen under their family names. On the other hand, *Chambers's Encyclopaedia, Chambers's Biographical Dictionary*, both the standard Peerages (*Burke* and *Debrett*), and *Kelly's Handbook to the Titled, Landed and Official Classes* use title for the chief entry, all but *Kelly* providing a cross-reference from the family name.

In a contribution to *The Indexer*[1] on this subject Mrs M. D. Anderson pointed out that the family-name method does possess the advantage of grouping together members of the same family who bore different titles and separating members of different families who bore the same title – the *DNB* includes fifteen Earls of Essex, belonging to eight different creations; it also avoids the difficulties caused by one man's bearing several successive titles – Sir Francis Bacon was created Baron Verulam in 1618 and Viscount St Albans two years later. She suggested a compromise: where the work in hand is meant for "specialist historians, genealogists, and

[1] Vol. 4, No. 2 (Autumn 1964), p. 51.

so forth", the chief entry should be under the surname (with a cross-reference from the title or titles), otherwise under title.

Where the title method, as recommended above, is adopted, the indexer should be careful to distinguish between different members of a line of hereditary peers by identifying the one concerned by his number and correct rank (Baron, Viscount, Earl, Marquis, Duke):

Home, 14th Earl of (later Sir Alec Douglas-Home)[1]
Salisbury, 3rd Marquis of

This does not apply, of course, when the one and only holder of a title has died without an heir or successor. But it does apply to a contemporary peer, since the indexer may hope that his index will outlive the nobleman concerned. In recent years an increasing number of life peers have been created; since they are invariably barons, they can be simply treated like this:

Hill of Luton, Lord

Bishops and Law Lords are Lords of Parliament (for their term of office) but are not peers; for the indexer's treatment of the former, see below.

There are exceptional cases where the bulk of a peer's life-work has been done before he was ennobled, so that his surname is far better known than his title, which may not even be mentioned in the text. The already mentioned Francis Bacon is one instance; others are Benjamin Disraeli (Earl of Beaconsfield) and Sidney Webb (1st Baron Passfield), while it may not be commonly known that Sir Robert and Horace Walpole became towards the end of their lives the 1st and 4th Earls of Orford respectively. In all such cases it is preferable to use the surname for the chief entry, cross-referring, when necessary, from the alternative title heading.

Saints and ecclesiastical dignitaries

A saint, unless more generally recognized (especially in the text)

---

[1] Sir Alec renounced his peerage in 1963 in order to become Prime Minister with a seat in the Commons. There should be a cross-reference from Douglas-Home. But if the text referred to present-day affairs, the procedure would have to be reversed, and Douglas-Home would become the principal heading. The name is pronounced "Hume", but that does not require a further cross-reference.

under some other title, is to be entered under his Christian name, followed by the word *Saint* (spelt out in full):

Boanerges (*see* James, Saint, *and* John, Saint)
Francis of Assisi, Saint
Francis Xavier, Saint
James, Saint, the Apostle
John, Saint, the Apostle
More, Sir Thomas
Thomas More, Saint, *see* More, Sir Thomas
Xavier, Saint Francis, *see* Francis Xavier

Where two people are mentioned in the text as having been canonized with the same name, they must be carefully distinguished in the index:

Augustine, Saint, Archbishop of Canterbury
Augustine, Saint, Bishop of Hippo

Popes and anti-popes are indexed under the pontifical names they have assumed. Should any be referred to in the text by his surname as Cardinal before being elected to the Holy See, that should receive a cross-reference from it:

Adrian IV, Pope (1154–9), the only English pope
Breakspear, Cardinal Nicholas, *see* Adrian IV
Gregory I, Pope (590–604)
    x Gregory, Saint[1]   ⎫ [if necessary]
    x Gregory the Great, Pope ⎭
Honorius II, Anti-pope (1061–4)
Paul VI, Pope (1963–78)

Archbishops, bishops and archdeacons should preferably be indexed under their surnames even if the text does not mention those but speaks of them only in connexion with their sees or archidiaconal districts. A suggested form of cross-reference might run something like this:

Canterbury, Archbishops of, *see* Davidson, Randall; Fisher of Lambeth, Lord; Lang of Lambeth, Lord; Temple, Frederick; *and* Temple, William

---

[1] Of the sixteen Popes Gregory, five have been canonized, including Gregory I.

Married women

The indexing treatment of their names will depend largely on the text. If the marriage takes place in the course of the narrative and relatively little is said of the lady's pre-marital circumstances, then it is best to make the main entry under her married name with a simple cross-reference from the maiden name. But if she remains single for the bulk of the book and then, as so often, fades out of the picture after her wedding, the process will have to be reversed and the maiden name will form the main entry. When the lady in question is herself the subject of the biography being indexed, or becomes married to its subject, and consequently there are numerous allusions to both her girlhood and her married life, I am disposed to treat the two states as separate existences in the index, linked by a "see also" or a "q.v." (see pp. 113–4) cross-reference, although this risks incurring a charge of "scattered information".

When a lady marries more than once, it is best to reserve the main entry for the final married name, unless it should happen that the bulk of the allusions concern a previous marriage and the last married name is only referred to casually, in which case the latter needs to be given a mere cross-reference entry. This might happen in the index to a book or periodical article dealing with Dr Johnson and his friend Mrs Thrale, who on the death of her brewer husband, to the lexicographer's disappointment, married the musician, Gabriel Piozzi:

Piozzi, Hester Lynch, *see* Thrale, Hester
Thrale, Hester Lynch (*née* Salusbury; later Mrs Piozzi)

It sometimes happens that, for professional or other reasons, a lady retains her maiden name after marriage and is usually referred to by that name; in such a case it should be used for the main entry, a cross-reference being given from the married name if that occurs in the text. Thus Dame Sybil Thorndike was married to the late Sir Lewis Casson, but who would dream of looking for her name under C?

Thorndike, Dame Sybil (Lady Casson)

If, after marriage, a lady couples her maiden name with that of her husband, the entry should be made under the latter, unless she chooses to hyphen the two names:

> Stowe, Harriet Beecher
>   *x* Beecher, Harriet [if the maiden name is alluded to in the text]

This rule does not apply to a woman whose language is Czech, Hungarian, Italian or Spanish, when the entry should always be made under the first surname.

Change of title or status

There are other people besides married women who may change their title or status in the course of a narrative. In such a case all the allusions should be grouped under one heading (preferably that having the latest title or term of address), the other titles, when necessary, being given as cross-references:

> George IV, King of Great Britain, Ireland and Hanover, 104–38
>   Prince of Wales, as, 87, 93
>   Prince Regent, as, 95, 98
> Prince Regent, the, *see* George IV
> Regent, the Prince, *see* George IV
> Wales, Prince of, *see* George IV

Non-surname headings

In addition to saints, popes, monarchs and nobility, there are some other instances where a name other than a surname is used for the keyword. The ancient Greeks and biblical characters, for example, had no surnames. Then again, the old chroniclers and other mediaeval characters are indexed under their Christian names:

> Geoffrey of Monmouth
> Hereward the Wake
> Jesus, *or* Jesus Christ, *or* Jesus of Nazareth
> John of Gaunt, Duke of Lancaster
>   *x* Lancaster, John of Gaunt, Duke of
> Moses
> Sophocles

Foreign personal names

Indexing and cataloguing are two distinct arts. But they have several rules in common, and one of them is the proper arrangement of foreign personal names. Consequently, for the following information I owe much to the *Anglo-American Cataloguing Rules* (British Text; The Library Association, 1967).[1] I am also indebted to Brigadier E. E. G. L. Searight, formerly the Indexer-in-Chief of *Keesing's Contemporary Archives* and author of the chapter on "Name Headings" in *Training in Indexing* (1969), for many useful hints.

European names. If we bear in mind the rule about compound names with prefixes, most European names are fairly straight-forward. The exceptions are: Spanish (including Latin-American names of Spanish origin); a few Portuguese; Hungarian; and some Russian.

Spanish (and more occasionally Portuguese and Brazilian) surnames often have the mother's name following that of the father, with sometimes a *y* (="and") between them. In all such cases the patronymic should be used for the keyword, followed by the other name. Thus, the Cuban dictator's name is actually Castro Ruz, but here "Castro, Dr Fidel" should suffice for the index heading, unless the text names him as "Castro Ruz".

In a Hungarian context the surname comes first (e.g. "Bartók Béla"), but in indexing this a comma will have to be inserted:

Bartók, Béla

Among Russian names the surnames Lenin (Vladimir Lenin), Trotsky (Leon Trotsky) and Stalin (Joseph Stalin) were all assumed ones, their actual born names being Ulyanov, Bronstein and Djugashvili respectively. These last should have no place in an index, unless expressly referred to in the text, and then only as cross-references. It should be noted that Stalin's daughter has written her books under the name of Svetlana Alliluyeva, her mother's surname, although she has been married more than once. Her maiden name was Svetlana Stalina, as Soviet women add *a* to their patronymics.

Arabic names. These can present some difficulty. In cases of doubt the indexer is advised to consult a reliable reference source. In

---

[1] A new edition of the *Rules*, with unified English and American text, was published late in 1978 while this book was in the press.

general they are to be indexed under the personal name:

> Faisal ibn ["the son of"] Abdul Aziz, King of Saudi Arabia
> Omar al Khayyam
> *x* Khayyam, Omar

When there are several personal or given names, the element should be chosen by which the character is best known. This may be an honorific compound of which the last part is *Al-Din*:

> Sadr Al-Din al-Qunawi, Muhammad ibn Ishaq
> *x* Muhammad ibn Ishaq

Or it may be a compound of which *Abu, Abd-el* or *Abdul* forms the first word:

> Abdul Kerim Pasha
> Abu Hayyan al-Tawhidi, Ali ibn Muhammad
> *x* Ali ibn Muhammad

Or a patronymic, starting with *Ibn*:

> Ibn Hisham, 'Abd al-Malik
> *x* 'Abd al-Malik

Or a descriptive epithet, sometimes indicating origin or residence:

> al-Bukhari, Muhammad ibn Ismail

On the other hand, many of the more sophisticated Arabs have adopted their final name as their surname, and this must be used by the indexer as his keyword:

> Boumedienne, Col. Houari
> Nasser, Gamal Abdel

But, as Searight points out, again there are exceptions; "that stormy petrel of Iraqi politics, Rashid Ali al Gailani, was always known as Rashid Ali and should be listed among the R's".[1]

Burmese names. The name should be entered in full without inver-

---

[1] *Training in Indexing*, p. 68.

sion, except that terms of address and any Western given name should be transposed to the end. Examples of Burmese terms of address are: *U* (the most frequent); *Daw* (female); *Maung*; and *Thakin*. Many Burmese names consist of only one element, like that of U Thant, the former Secretary-General of the United Nations:

Ba U, *U*
Mya Shein, *Daw*
Thant, *U*
  x U Thant

Chinese names. These are normally easy enough for the indexer to handle. Each person has a surname (usually of one syllable) and a personal name (often of two hyphened syllables) and, as in the written form the surname comes first, the index heading consists of the name as it stands:

Chou En-lai
Mao Tse-tung

More occasionally such forms as the following appear:

Hu Wei
Lee Kuan Yew
Ssu-ma Ch'ien

where "Hu", "Lee" and "Ssu-ma" are the surnames.

Some very modern Chinese with Western ties have adopted the Western practice of putting their family names last. These must be inverted:

Soong, T. V.

Care must be taken when the keyword contains a consonant followed by an apostrophe, which affects the pronunciation. So "Tang" and "T'ang" must be kept distinct in indexing, as also "Tsa" and "Ts'a".

The emperors' names usually encountered in European literature are the "reign titles", which were used for whole reigns after 1368. Such names as K'ang-hsi and Chien-lung are of this type and must be indexed as they stand. Chinese titles and ranks are usually translated in European books and in any case are unlikely to occur in a way likely to be mistaken for part of the name.

An authoritative article by H. D. Talbot on the subject of indexing Chinese names was published in *The Indexer*,[1] and this forms the basis of the above information.

Korean, Vietnamese, Cambodian and Laotian names, so much in the news in recent years, generally follow the same pattern as Chinese names. But one or two snags have to be watched for. As Searight points out, "unfortunately for the indexer, the South Koreans (probably owing to American contacts) are now beginning to westernize their names and place the family name last".[2] A few years ago *The Times* stated that Tong Won Lee and Choong Hoeng Park were visiting this country. Previously these men had normally been referred to as Lee Tong Won and Park Choong Hoeng. Again, "especially in South Vietnam, Laos and Cambodia, celebrities are customarily referred to by one of their personal names only".[3] Thus, the former Vice-President and Prime Minister of South Vietnam, Air Vice-Marshal Nguyen Cao Ky, has "Nguyen" as his family name but is almost invariably referred to as "Marshal Ky". Again, the family name of Cambodia's Prince Norodom Sihanouk is "Norodom", which should, strictly, be used as the keyword. In the same way, General Lon Nol would be rightly indexed under "Lon".

The safest plan in such cases is to consult such authorities as an international dictionary of biography, or *Whitaker's Almanack*, or the *Statesman's Year Book*, or the Name Index to *Keesing's Contemporary Archives*, as appropriate, and to be plentiful with cross-references. In the absence of such source information it may be possible to query the author of the text as to which of various names is the surname and whether it is right to use that name for the keyword.

It should be noted that the following two Laotian "names" are actually terms of address: "Chiao"; "Tiao".

Indian names. The indexing of an Indian name may vary according to the period in which its owner flourished, or according to his

---

[1] Vol. 2, No. 3 (Spring 1961), pp. 99–103.
[2] *Training in Indexing*, p. 65.   [3] Ibid.

religion or language. Early names, that is up to the middle of the nineteenth century, should be entered under the first word of the name.

More modern names, if of Muslims (whether Pakistani or not), ought to come (like the Arabic names above) under their personal names:

Ayub Khan

But many Indian Muslims have found it convenient to adopt a surname and, when this is so, that should form the keyword, since the good indexer always defers to a name-owner's own preference:

Vakil, Mohammed Ali

Modern Hindus usually use their final names as surnames, sometimes in compound form:

Gandhi, "Mahatma" Mohandas
Krishna Menon, V. K.
  x Menon, V. K. Krishna
Nehru, Jawaharlal

The final name may be a caste name, e.g. Rao. But these caste names are not always used as surnames. A preceding name may be chosen instead. This, if known, should be made the keyword. Otherwise use the last name. Names in four Indian languages (Kannada, Malayalam, Tamil and Telugu), however, often take the form of three words: the name of the place of ancestral residence (or more rarely, the father's given name); the given name; the caste name. There being no surname, the second or given name will have to be used to start the heading:

Sankaran Nair, *Sir* Chettur

Sikhs do not use their final name, their generic Sikh name (normally Singh), as a surname, and must be listed under their first or personal name:

Ranjit Singh

They sometimes, however, use clan names as surnames: Ahlve-walia, Badal, Garewal and Sethi are examples. In such cases they should be indexed under the clan name, followed by the personal name:

    Badal, Prakash Singh

Indonesian names. The true Indonesian has but one element in his name and so is easy for the indexer:

    Sukarno, Dr
      x Soekarno

But there are also Indonesians bearing Arabic, Chinese, Dutch, Indian, Javanese, Sumatran and Malayan names; these should be indexed under the last of their names. An exception is those Chinese Indonesians whose surname comes first in the written form of their names; these should be treated without inversion or comma.

Occasionally the name's owner regards the penultimate element of his name as part of his surname, and then that element must be made the keyword:

    Bin Nuh, Abdullah
      x Nuh, Abdullah Bin

Indonesian terms of address are very numerous – too many to be listed here. The *Anglo-American Cataloguing Rules* recommend that the following be *not* included in headings:

bung (=brother)	njonja (=mistress)
empu (=mister)	nona (=miss)
engku (=mister)	pak (=father)
entjik (=mister or mistress)	tuan (=mister)
ibu (=mother)	wan (=mister)

Japanese names. The Japanese names likely to be encountered by the indexer nearly all comprise but two elements: a single forename followed by the family name. For indexing, these must be inverted:

    Koga, Admiral Mineichi

Thai (Siamese) names. Surnames became required by law in Thailand in 1915. The Thai's surname is his last one, and that is the keyword one. When he has a title of nobility or honour conferred on him (e.g. Krom, Phra or Somdet) there is also bestowed a special name that replaces his old name. The special name becomes the keyword, followed by the title(s). A Buddhist priest of Thailand is to be indexed under his religious name, followed by his title of nobility (if any) as well as his ecclesiastical title, the latter coming last:

Vamarat, Somdet Phra Sankarat

Tibetan names. Searight made a special study of the indexing of Tibetan names[1] after the flight of the Dalai Lama in 1959. Most of them are composite, and he found that "more often than not, most of the components of a name represented offices held or honorific titles. These might be combined with place-names of monasteries or districts, with the names of noble families or with an individual's personal name." He decided that the keyword for a Tibetan "should be his personal name or the name of the noble family to which he belonged; failing that, the name of his monastery or the district he governed; and that all titles and offices should be subordinated to these names".

GEOGRAPHICAL NAMES

Within the limitations laid down on p. 52, nearly every geographical name mentioned in the text is indexable. The test is whether or not some pertinent statement is made about it. Something has already been said about the indexing of place-names in the section on "Inverted headings" (Chapter 3); there can be no excuse for listing the main entry for "The People's Republic of China" under P. Similarly "County Clare" should be indexed as "Clare, County (Republic of Ireland)". The parenthesized qualification is necessary, as explained below, because there are other Clares ("homonyms") in Suffolk and South Australia.

---

[1] *The Indexer,* Vol. 3, No. 2 (Autumn 1962), pp. 64–6. This article contains some useful examples of personal and family names, and of those of noble families and monasteries.

Foreign place-names

A geographical name may have more than one form – its own
national form and those used by people in other countries. Thus,
the seaport the British call Flushing is known to the French as
Flessingue and to the Dutch and Germans as Vlissingen. The
indexer must employ the form used in the text, which, if the book
be a British (or American) one, will almost certainly be the English
form; he need cross-refer from the national form only if that also
occurs in the text.

Identification of names

The index-user must be left in no doubt as to the location of the
various villages, towns, cities and other communities whose names
are listed in the index. This is especially important when there
exists in some part of the world another place bearing the same
name, in other words a homonym. The identification can best be
made by the addition of the name of the county, *arrondissement*,
state or province in which the place is situated, together with any
further distinction necessary, and with any cross-reference that
may be needed on account of text mentions:

    Baltimore, Cork (Eire)
    Baltimore, Md (USA)

    Bath, Jamaica
    Bath, Netherlands
    Bath, Avon (England)

    Washington, DC
    Washington, Tyne & Wear (England)
    Washington, *State* (USA)

  But in a text dealing with England alone, the heading "Cambridge" would be sufficient unless its Massachusetts counterpart
also happened to be referred to.

Incidental place-names

A geographical name is sometimes encountered as the distinguishing term of some product, e.g. Plaster of Paris, or Chile saltpetre.
Only when the place-name comes first in the expression does it
need to be used as a keyword. "Plaster of Paris" can be indexed

solely as it stands. "Chile saltpetre" would require a further entry under "Sodium nitrate" and perhaps others under "Caliche" and "Saltpetre".

Preliminary expressions

When a geographical name starts with "Bay of", "Cape" (or "Cape of"), "Gulf of", "Isle of", "Lake", "Mount", or "Sea of", and those terms actually describe their function, then the whole expression must be inverted and the proper name becomes the keyword:

> Biscay, Bay of, Atlantic Ocean
> Gris Nez, Cape, France
> Marmara, Sea of, Turkey
> Mexico, Gulf of, America
> Nyasa, Lake, East Africa
> Olives, Mount of, Palestine
> Wight, Isle of, England

More rarely, however, the first element is regarded as a relevant part of the complete name, in which case the first word *can* become the keyword:

> Cape of Good Hope, South Africa
>   x Good Hope, Cape of
> Lake of the Woods, Canada/USA
>   x Woods, Lake of the

Also, the first element *must* supply the keyword and the whole expression remains uninverted when one of the geographical terms in the preceding paragraph ("Bay", "Cape", etc.) forms the start of the name of a city or town or island or anything but what it affects to describe:

> Bay Island, Honduras   [island]
> Lake City, South Carolina   [town]
> Lake District, the   [region]
> Mount Allison University, New Brunswick
> Mount Morgan, Queensland   [town]
> Mount Palomar Observatory, California
> Sea Island, Georgia (USA)   [island]
> Sea Lake, Victoria (Australia)   [town]

Names prefixed by definite article

Where it is the English definite article, it should be inverted for indexing purposes – Hague, The. (But the *Oxford Atlas* gives double entry for The Vale, New South Wales, that is under inverted and uninverted forms.) With foreign articles there is no inversion in an English index:

> El Dorado (mythical land of gold)
> Le Havre (France)
>   x Havre, Le
> Los Angeles, California
> 's-Gravenhage, Netherlands

Note, however, that El Salvador, Republica de, is most often indexed as Salvador.

CHAPTER FIVE
Subject Headings

Order and simplification are the first steps towards mastery of a
subject – the actual enemy is the unknown.

Thomas Mann (1875–1955),
The Magic Mountain (1924)

"Subject" has a very wide connotation and could be taken to
comprise all items of reading matter, including proper names. The
subject of a book or periodical article is what is discussed or dealt
with therein. But throughout this work a "subject heading", as
opposed to a proper-name heading, has the meaning of a heading
which points to a common noun or to an abstract noun – perhaps
a concept or condition or activity – or else is an expression coined
to give the gist of some statement in the material indexed. In
neither case does its keyword normally start with a capital letter.

A few publishers sometimes prefer their indexes to be confined
to entries for the names of persons and places. This practice – due
probably to motives of economy (or, as some people would label
it, of parsimony) – is rarely justified. If the purpose of providing a
book (or a periodical) with an index is to enable its users to locate
its contents, then topics and concepts are just as likely to be sought
as proper names. For instance, in any book concerned with British
statecraft immediately prior to World War II the index's omission
of the subject heading "appeasement" would be unthinkable, as
similarly would be the absence of "apartheid" from the index to a
book on South African politics.

Selection of subject headings
In many cases, however, subject headings present far more difficulty than do proper-name headings both in their selection and in

their treatment. The entire usefulness of an index is largely determined by the suitability of the subject headings that have been
chosen. Proper-name headings can as a rule be entered in only
one way, but the selection of subject-headings often involves much
discretion and caution and sometimes a measure of standardization.

This difficulty is due to some extent to the fact that, as already
pointed out in Chapter 1, there are two quite distinct types of index
user,[1] both of whom have constantly to be kept in mind. The
person who has already read through the text may be presumed to
be familiar with its author's style of terminology and consequently
to know under what index heading to look in order to find some
topic about which he wishes to refresh his memory. Far less easy
to cater for is the person who has not read through the text (and
probably has no intention of doing so) but merely wishes to consult
it to discover what (if anything) it has to say about some particular
subject. An especial difficulty arises from the possibility – in some
cases the probability – that he may be thinking of that subject
matter by some quite different name or term from that used in the
text and consequently also as a heading in the index. Hence it may
often be necessary to introduce cross-references from familiar
expressions that do not appear in the text to those that do (e.g.
from Farming to Agriculture). This problem is further discussed
below in the section on "Vocabulary control".

The actual selection (already dealt with to some extent in
Chapter 3), which can be carried out at the same time as that of the
proper-name headings, must be made during a careful scanning of
the text. This scanning constitutes the key operation in indexing.
The headings that suggest themselves can be inserted in the margin
of the text or even (subject to later editing and revision) taken
direct onto the cards.

The titles of chapters and sections and of periodical articles form
an obvious quarry. But, if the index is to be at all comprehensive,

---

[1] That there is also a third type of index-user was suggested by Mr Richard Bird
in a training-course lecture given under the auspices of the Society of Indexers –
namely, a person who is searching for ideas or inspiration: "Some people, particularly students, browse through an index for odd aspects of a subject which had not
occurred to them before." Akin to this type of index-browser is the literary critic.
Such people undoubtedly exist, but I do not think that the indexer need exercise his
mind unduly on their account.

the subject headings must by no means be confined to them; there will be words, expressions, phrases and statements of importance in the text that also need to be indexed. In the case of chapter and section titles, it is not necessarily their actual wording so much as the substance of what follows that will determine the form of the subject headings. Thus, in a descriptive volume on the Scilly Islands there is a chapter entitled "Fish, Flesh and Flowers". But this has been very properly rejected by the indexer in favour of four subject headings:

> Birds of Scilly, 133–5
> Fauna of Scilly, 128–33
> Fishing off Scilly, 135–8
> Flora of Scilly, 138–42

Again, an author may try to provide a mildly facetious title. Unless this happens to be some particularly memorable phrase that might be looked for in the index, the wise indexer is advised to steer clear. Thus, some years ago *The Economist* had an article ingeniously entitled "The Old Lady Shows her Amber". One can imagine many an indexer painstakingly indexing this under O, under L and under A. But his labour would be in vain. For "Amber" was a reference to traffic lights, "Old Lady" to her of Threadneedle Street, and the subject was the raising of the bank rate! All that was needed was one subject heading under B.

As regards the important "words, expressions, phrases and statements" picked from the text for inclusion in the index, a single word will usually speak for itself and can as a rule be used in its text form as a subject heading – not, of course, as a simple heading but accompanied by its description or *raison d'être*, as a qualification or modification. Frequently the two elements of the entry call for inversion:

> Currency, decimal
> Education, higher
> Dogs, gestation period of
> Wisdom, statuary group representing

Of the above examples, the first two would probably require uninverted headings (under "Decimal" and "Higher" respectively) as well, while the third, the "Dogs" heading, should find no place at all as such in any book devoted wholly to the canine species. The heading would have to be "Gestation period".

These compound subject headings can be fairly formidable. Dr Michael Lynch cites[1] the following passage in the text of the American *Chemical Abstracts*:

> Durabolin protection against metabolism of calcium by bones after administration of cortisone and its analogs in bone disorders.

Out of the no fewer than nine substantives in that passage, "Calcium" is chosen as the keyword of the chief heading, although there are four other words – Durabolin, metabolism, cortisone and bone (disorders) – that deserve at least to be cross-referred from. The keyword has no qualification but there are a number of modifying components which must be included in the heading. The complete index entry runs as follows:

> Calcium, metabolism of, by bones, after administration of cortisone and its analogs, durabolin protection against, in bone disorders, 60; 16173b

An equally exhaustive and even neater entry could, I suggest, have been the following:

> Calcium, Durabolin protection against bone metabolism of, after administration of cortisone and its analogs in bone disorders.

Note the position of the punctuation, all-important in this context.

Vocabulary control

"The question of deciding what is or is not significant [and therefore indexable] is the most pervasive unsolved problem of indexing at every level."[2] But, once having decided what are the significant items for our subject headings, the next question arises: how shall we word those subject headings? As already hinted, the keyword will often be a word used by the author. What happens, however, if one is indexing a work by many authors, some of whom use

---

[1] Michael F. Lynch, "Computer-organised Display of Subject Information", *The Indexer*, Vol. 7, No. 3 (Spring 1971), pp. 94–100.
[2] Eric J. Coates, "Scientific and Technical Indexing, II", *Training in Indexing*, p. 130.

different terms to express the same object or concept? Which is
one to adopt for the chief subject heading and which for the cross-
references? A similar difficulty occurs in bibliographical indexing.
The answer must surely lie in referring to some authority, preferably a manual of vocabulary control. Attempts have been made,
particularly in scientific fields, to standardize the terminology.
Where they have failed to catch on, it is because the recommended
products are not in accordance with conventional preference,
so that simpler, more familiar terms continue to be used in
literature.

There are, however, a number of thesauri, dictionaries of
synonyms and collections of technical trade terms which are
available in many public reference libraries and can be of considerable assistance to the indexer who is seeking alternative or related
expressions. (I am not for one moment suggesting that he should
consult one of these authority lists for every subject heading he
may wish to use – that would indeed involve a prodigious waste
of time – but only in cases of doubt or difficulty.) For general
literature there are, for instance, the invaluable Roget's *Thesaurus
of English Words and Phrases*, and Sears' *List of Subject Headings*
(10th edn, New York, 1972) as well as Oliver Stonor's *First Book
of Synonyms* (1963) and Roget's *International Thesaurus* (1962) and
Webster's *New Dictionary of Synonyms* (Springfield, Mass., 1968).
Another very useful reference tool is the latest edition of the
Library of Congress Subject Headings. But the usage to be found in
this, as well as in Sears and Webster, is American and consequently
not in every case the same as the British. The same caution applies
to many of the specialized thesauri mentioned in the next paragraph.

There are several thesauri covering particular subject fields, the
following being just a few examples: *Thesaurus of Engineering and
Scientific Terms* (New York: Engineers' Joint Council, 1967);
Medical Subject Headings (MeSH) (Bethesda, Maryland: National
Library of Medicine, annual); John F. Blagden's *Management In-
formation Retrieval: a new indexing language* (London: Management
Publications, 2nd edn, 1971); *NCC Thesaurus of Computing Terms*
(Manchester: National Computing Centre, 1972, 2 vols); *Engineer-
ing Index Thesaurus* (New York: CCM Information Corporation,
1972); and *Thesaurus of ERIC Descriptors* (New York: Macmillan
Information; London: Collier-Macmillan, 5th edn, 1974).

A word of caution is necessary regarding the use of these aids. The indexer must be careful to ensure that any related expression that he picks up from one of them to use as a cross-reference or as a subject-heading bears exactly the same shade of meaning as the text expression that he is trying to index.

Synonyms and other related subject headings

Strictly a synonym is "a word or phrase identical and co-extensive in sense and usage with another of the same language" (e.g. kingly, royal and regal; or "heliotherapy" and "treatment of disease by exposure to ultraviolet radiation"). But such cases are comparatively rare and *The Concise Oxford Dictionary* allows also for the looser meaning of a word "equivalent to another in some only of either's senses"; every ship is a vessel but not every vessel is a ship.

Some of the reasons for having sometimes to insert separate subject headings (usually cross-reference entries) for synonyms to keywords already given a place in the index have been set out in the previous section and a few titles of books to be consulted for suitable synonyms have been suggested.

The extent of the use of synonyms, as well as the choice between them, will depend to some extent on the class of reader for whom the publication is intended; a general (as opposed to a specialist) reader of a book dealing with meteorology is far more apt to look for "rainfall" than "precipitation". But even with specialist words and expressions the terminology in current use is far from being standardized and there still is a great lack of uniformity.

If synonyms occur in the text, it is bad practice to distribute the page references among them in the index, for this leads to "scattered information" – an unforgivable sin on the part of any indexer. Thus, the following simply will not do:

Aliens, 23–7, 59
Foreigners, 62, 163

One of the synonyms must be chosen for the complete entry and the other(s) linked to it by means of "see" cross-references:

Aliens, 23–7, 59, 62, 163, 187
   hostility to, 28–9, 188
Foreigners, *see* Aliens

(The question of how many references are allowable in any entry without recourse to sub-entries is dealt with in Chapter 6.)

In order to constitute synonyms, words must be equivalents, that is to say, not only must keyword A include the meaning of keyword B, but B must also include the meaning of A. Sometimes, as Vickery[1] points out, D, which includes the meanings of A, B, C, etc., will be used as a subject heading. In this case D will probably be a generic term and the species A, B, C, etc. will be merely related to it and neither synonyms of it nor of themselves. A generic term should not be given a separate heading unless it is specifically alluded to in the text. Take, for example, the word "metals". If it has its own significant references in the text, it might have some such entry as the following in an index:

Metals (*see also* Copper; Gold; Iron; Silver), 85–9, 113, 218

In the above entry the subordinates Copper, Gold, etc. are related headings; they do *not* require to be cross-referred to one another (e.g. Gold to Silver and vice versa). The great distinction here between synonyms and other forms of related headings is that, whereas with synonyms each except the chosen entry becomes what has been called a "rejected heading" and must have a "see" cross-reference, the other related headings become full entries in their own right and are linked by "see also" cross-references (or sometimes by a "q.v." – see pp. 113–4); certain exceptions, when a "see" cross-reference is needed, are noted on pp. 94 and 110.

In addition to synonyms, generic terms and subordinates, as instanced above, there are several other kinds of related headings similarly requiring "see also" cross-references. Attempts have been made with varying success to classify the different categories, but such a classification (even if it could meet with general concurrence) would be of more assistance to the compiler of a subject catalogue than to the indexer for whom the present work is intended. Mention must be made, however, of the commonest kind, the co-ordinates,[2] that is to say, words and expressions of equal status, each having some compelling association with one (or occasionally

---

[1] B. C. Vickery, *On Retrieval System Theory* (2nd edn, 1963), p. 35.
[2] Not to be confused with "Co-ordinate indexing", a method devised and so named by Mortimer Taube, but admittedly of very limited applicability to book indexing.

more) of the others. When these co-ordinates are themselves significantly alluded to in the text, the cross-references used must be "see also" ones; but where they are merely inserted in the index for the convenience of the user, a single "see" cross-reference for the co-ordinate only must suffice. Thus, to go back to the "Aliens" entry above, the index to an appropriate publication might contain the following subject entries:

> Aliens (*see also* Immigrants *and* Strangers), 23–7, 59, 62, 165, 186
> Foreigners, *see* Aliens
> Immigrants (*see also* Aliens *and* Strangers), 75–83, 89
> Outlanders, *see* Aliens
> Strangers (*see also* Aliens *and* Immigrants), 256

In the above list the second and fourth are synonymous headings, the remainder related co-ordinate headings. Further examples of associated co-ordinates can be brought to mind in abundance, e.g.:

> Air: Heat; Pressure; Temperature; Tempests; Wind
> Man: Anthropometry; Anthropology; Anthropomorphism; Males; Moon, man in the; Moon, men on the; etc.

It will be found, however, in practice, that in a normal index, owing to considerations of space, the number of such related headings that can be used in any one case, although not themselves specifically and significantly alluded to in the text, is strictly limited. They should not be used, therefore, unless definitely likely to be sought by the inquirer.

Other types of related headings include two concerned with figures of speech – synecdoche and metonymy. A synecdoche occurs in the text where either (a) a species is named having the meaning of the whole genus, or else (b) the genus is named for a species. Examples of (a) are: "bread" for food in general; pounds, shillings and pence (before the introduction of decimal currency) for wealth or riches generally; "hands" for crew. For (b) can be cited the use of "the telephone" when only part of the apparatus is intended, for instance, the receiver. Metonymy is the substitution of an attribute or adjunct for that of the thing meant, as with the crown for the king or queen – we speak of "Crown lands", while *Rex* v. *Philpott* is referred to as a "Crown prosecution". This meaning is so commonly employed as to render "Crown" in this sense an acceptable subject heading in an index, in its own right.[1]

Antonyms

An antonymous expression has been defined as a word or phrase of contrary meaning to another; consequently "Synonyms and antonyms" forms a good example of its meaning. Other examples: Vivisection and anti-vivisection; Activator and inhibitor; Bliss and woe ("A bliss in proof, and proved, a very woe" – Shakespeare's Sonnet No. 129).

An antonym can, of course, be given its own full subject entry, merely linked by "see also" cross-references to and from the subject entry of which it forms the opposite. But if this involves splitting the page references between the two, it is usually infinitely preferable to combine them under one heading, e.g.:

    Anti-friction devices, *see* Friction
    Anti-vivisection, *see* Vivisection
    Friction and anti-friction devices
    Vivisection and anti-vivisection

The same result can sometimes be achieved – and perhaps made clearer to the user – by turning the antonym into a subheading:

    Friction, 47, 83, 112–31
        devices against, 123, 127–31

Care must be taken, when combining an antonym and its opposite in one compound heading, to ensure that the two parts are exact opposites. "Employment and unemployment" would pass muster, but Cyclone and Anticyclone are not true antonyms, nor are Toxin and Antitoxin. Again, "Monarchy and republicanism" would scarcely be a suitable heading (unless such forms the title of a periodical article or of a chapter or section in a book), since there are other constitutional alternatives to monarchy, not to mention the Republican Party in the USA.

---

[1] If "crown" is also used in the same book or periodical article in its literal sense of a regal head-covering, then both become homonyms and require separate headings:

    Crown (regal governing power)
    crown (regal head-covering)

Homonyms

Great care must be taken to distinguish homonymous keywords, that is to say two or more words having the same form but distinct meanings. Such words should always be given separate entries and not grouped under one heading, as in so many dictionaries. Each should be given a brief parenthesized explanation or else differentiated by turning it into a compound expression. Take as an example the word "cocoa". In one and the same volume the single word may be used in the sense of the seed or bean; of cocoa crops; of the trees; and of the finished product:

> Cacao, *see* Cocoa beans; Cocoa crops *and* Cocoa trees
> Cocoa (hot drink)
> Cocoa beans
> Cocoa crops
> Cocoa powder
> Cocoa trees

Other examples:

> Notes (annotation)
> Notes (brief missives)
> Notes (in music)
> Notes (record)
>
> Perches (fresh-water fish)
> Perches (horizontal bars)
> Perches (units of measurement)

Classified or specific headings?

This is a matter that has provoked a certain amount of controversy. It is possible that, in introducing classification for their subject headings, indexers may have been influenced by the example of the many classified subject catalogues (themselves in form indexes), of which the one compiled for the British Museum (now the British Library) is the most noteworthy. But should, for instance, an index contain one general entry for Astronomy, to which the user must turn for any information he may be seeking on the sun, the moon or the planets, or on Copernicus, Galileo or Newton? Or again, should there be a main heading for Schools, with the following sub-entries: approved; comprehensive; denominational; grammar; preparatory; primary; public; secondary; special? That latter example would be a typical case of classification and might well come about as a result of the indexer's having lit upon a whole chapter with the title "Schools" in the text; he uses the word for his entry heading and then follows the various sections for his sub-entries, merely adapting the order alphabetically. That is poor indexing, especially if approved schools, comprehensive schools, etc., are not given separate entries; for those are the most likely headings to be sought.

This, then, is the dilemma which bedevils much classified indexing. Either we must repeat the sub-entries in full in their own separate entries, involving double entry, which, with one important exception (see p. 111), is to be deprecated as wasting precious space; or else we must treat Approved schools etc. as "rejected headings" (p. 93) – Approved schools, *see* Schools. But this runs directly counter to what, if not exactly a rule, is at least an established tradition of indexing, namely that cross-references should be downward from the general to the particular (or species), rather than the reverse.

I venture to suggest that the best way of resolving the dilemma is by completely declassifying the Schools entry:

Schools, kinds of, described, 239–57
Secondary schools, 241–6
Special schools, 254–7

And so with the rest of the former class subheadings. That would constitute indexing by *specific entry*, for which personally I would plump, rather than for classification, every time. Of course, if some or all of the kinds of school are significantly alluded to outside the page references given above for Schools, then the last-named heading would have to be modified by the addition of a cross-reference:

Comprehensive schools, 248–52, 317, 363
Grammar schools, 246–8, 317
Schools (*see also* Comprehensive *and* Grammar schools), kinds of, described, 239–57

It may be asked: If Approved schools, etc. are not to appear as modifications of the generic subject heading "Schools" except by way of "see also" cross-references, how is the often vast number of subheadings to be accounted for in the best indexes? The answer is surely that each one of the modifications and qualifications which form those subheadings is (or should be) an *aspect* of the subject heading, not a *species* of it. Thus, the following would be quite satisfactory:

Schools
    legislation concerning
    literature on
    teachers' salaries in, *see* Teachers
    teaching methods in

Here all the subheadings form different aspects of schools. It is important, therefore, to distinguish between aspects and species of a generic subject heading.

Advocates of classification have objected that specific entry indexing causes a proliferation of cross-references. But even a classified index will not be able to dispense entirely with that useful (and indeed essential) adjunct, only in this case many of the cross-references will have to be upward from the particular to the general. A great disadvantage of classification is that it tends to multiply the number of sub- and sub-subheadings.

The use of such sub-sub-divisions is a practice to be avoided, wherever possible, in all indexes (save perhaps those to legal textbooks); and is quite impossible where subheadings are "run-on". Their elimination can usually be managed by the simple device of turning the offending subheading into a cross-reference to a separate heading, with its own subheadings. Thus:

Not

Schools
    teachers' salaries in
      antedating of
      "Burnham scale" for
      strikes over

but

Schools
    teachers' salaries in,
      see Teachers' salaries

and

Teachers' salaries
    antedating of
    "Burnham scale" for
    strikes over

An indexer may well raise the question: "To what degree am I expected to extend specificity?" John Metcalfe[1] instances the

---

[1] *Information Indexing and Subject Cataloguing* (New York, 1957), para. 843.

possibility of such a heading as "Model T Ford Motor Car" (and touchingly quotes Falstaff: "Mistress Ford! I have had ford enough; I was thrown into the ford; I have my belly full of ford"). I suggest that in a book devoted wholly to motors the above instance might form a suitable index heading. But common sense imposes a limit to the degree of specificity and in a volume of more general literature the indexer might have to invert it into "Ford motors, Model T", and he could plead in extenuation that it is not necessary to descend to the *infima species* and that in any case Model T is a variety rather than a species (in the non-biological sense). But if, in these circumstances, he decides to make a separate heading for Model T, it should certainly have a reference to it from under Ford motors, unless both are alluded to only on the same page or in the same paragraph.

Again, Flying saucers and Gastric juices both form indexable items as they stand, and no heading will be required for either saucers or juices. But what if they are referred to in the text rather more specifically as "circular flying saucers" and "digestive gastric juices"? Similar decisions will have to be made as in the preceding paragraph. I suggest that "circular" and "digestive" can be treated as mere aspects or qualifications, and so should be inverted: Flying saucers, circular. The test is, under what heading is the user most likely to look?

Many of the principles I have tried to enunciate in this chapter can be found exemplified in the admirable index to John Horner's *Cataloguing* (1970). The indexer, who must surely be the author himself, supplies full preliminary notes in the form of an Introduction (to the index), occupying over a page and followed by an explanatory list of "Abbreviations used in the Index and the Text". The Introduction states:

> Specific entries are used, usually in direct phrase form, e.g. PHYSICAL FORMS OF CATALOGUES, not CATALOGUES: PHYSICAL FORMS.
> *See also* references are made from broader headings to more specific headings stage by stage, and between other headings having something in common.
> *See* references are made, where considered necessary, from unused, e.g. synonymous, forms to the form of heading used.

So much for specific entry, which, I suggest, is the method to be aimed at in the indexing of subject headings and indeed in all indexes in general. As regards classified entries, Dr J. E.

Holmstrom[1] comments: "If what ought to be a straight alphabetical sequence of terms denoting different things is interrupted
by pockets of attempted systematic classification of the things
themselves – 'concealed classifications' as they have aptly been
called – the only effect is to bewilder the user of the index by
leaving him in doubt as to where he ought to look for what he
wants."

None the less, two authors have recommended classification
schemes (but not classified entries) as an aid to the indexer. Derek
Langridge[2] suggests that after one reading of the text the indexer
should start by constructing the outline of a classified pattern on
the basis of the work; "the process consists of recognizing categories of terms and relationships between them". Again, Collison[3]
considers that to glance at an established classification scheme
(such as appropriate tables of the Dewey Decimal classification or
the Library of Congress classification) can be of great value in the
editing of indexes to highly detailed works on the more recondite
subjects. By doing so the indexer is able to reassure himself that
he has fully covered all the aspects and accepted terminology of
his subject. In addition to the two works named by Collison some
of those mentioned earlier in this chapter may be found useful.
But on this topic I speak as one not having authority (and not as
the scribes), for alas! I have no personal experience of either
Langridge's or Collison's method.

---

[1] *Training in Indexing*, p. 119.   [2] Ibid., p. 82.
[3] Robert L. Collison, *Indexes and Indexing* (4th edn, 1972), p. 97.

CHAPTER SIX
References and Cross-references

And the smooth stream in smoother numbers flows.
Alexander Pope (1688–1744),
An Essay on Criticism

By "smoother numbers" Pope presumably meant verses rather than page references, but the line seems equally applicable to a well-constructed index. The matter of inserting references after a heading and its subheadings (if any) to complete the entry is usually straightforward enough. There are, however, one or two rules to observe and a snag or two to heed.

To what do references refer?

In probably nine out of ten books the index reference is to the text's page number – sometimes called the "folio". (For the index references of periodicals and newspapers see Chapters 8 and 9.) But it can also refer to numbered paragraphs, numbered sections and other divisions of a book. Whenever the index references are to paragraphs or any division of the text other than pages it is essential that this be explained in a preliminary note (see pp. 165–6) before the start of the index proper; e.g. "References are to numbered paragraphs, *not* to page numbers". Sometimes this warning is regarded as so important that it is inserted in bold type at the bottom of every right-hand page of the index. But doing that means either that the indexer will have to sacrifice a couple of lines of his index on each of those pages or else that the publisher must pay a little extra to have the warning printed in the bottom margin.

Where a book consists of sections or paragraphs numbered consecutively throughout the text, a single numeral can suffice for each reference. But where each chapter has a fresh sequence of numbers for its sections, then the reference must start with the chapter number followed by a decimal point and the number of the section within the chapter (e.g. V.18, signifying the 18th section in Chapter V). If it is in a subsection or even a further subdivision that the item referred to is to be found, then that also must be noted in the index (e.g. V.18 (iv) or V.18 (g.3.ii)).

It is in a textbook (such as the present author immodestly trusts that *Indexing, The Art of* may become) that numbered paragraphs are most commonly used.[1] As providing reference numbers they possess two considerable advantages. First, paragraphs are almost invariably far less extensive than the printed matter on a whole page, so that the index-user will find it that much simpler to find any items he is seeking. Secondly, from the point of view of the indexer, the presence of numbered paragraphs throughout a book means that he need not wait for the printed page proofs in order to start his work; he can make a complete index from the manuscript itself or from the galley proofs (when the present-day publisher makes these available), provided he takes care to heed any material omissions or corrections affecting his index which are made by the author at a later stage. In this way, time may be saved in the production of the book. Against these advantages, two drawbacks must be weighed. First, paragraphs are almost invariably more numerous than pages, so that the number of paragraphs in a book of quite ordinary size may run into four figures, which may add to the length of the index. Second, and more important, because paragraphs are not of uniform length and thus not uniformly distributed through the book, they are more difficult for the index-user to locate than pages.

Paragraph numbers are usually printed (sometimes in boldface type) in the left-hand margin of the text opposite the first line of the paragraph. Occasionally they appear in ordinary type as part of the text at the end of the last line of the paragraph. In that way they appear less conspicuous, but are apt to be overlooked.

Sequences of reference numbers

Where the continuous treatment of an indexable item in the text

---

[1] Indeed, in a few modern textbooks, such as Herbert Rees's *Rules of Printed English* (1970), the text pages are left unnumbered throughout.

extends beyond a single page or paragraph (according to which system of reference numbers is being used), a group reference is called for, consisting of the first and last reference number, separated by an en rule or dash (e.g. 143–5).

The basic rule for such group references is to use the least number of digits possible:

8–9; 23–7; 142–5; 146–51; 1,753–6; 1,792–801; 2,997–3,014

(It may be observed that the pagination of single-volume publications rarely reaches the thousand-page mark, except in such works as *The Concise Oxford Dictionary* or *Debrett's Peerage*. But in multi-volume works, e.g. encyclopaedias, it sometimes runs to several thousands.)

In his useful *Rules of Printed English* (1970) Herbert Rees states that there is an exception to the above rule – "the figure 1 in teens must always be repeated" (214–16, *not* 214–6). I have encountered printers who always abide by this exception, even amending my "copy" in appropriate places. The book gives no reason for treating teens differently from other numerals, but Mr Rees has himself given me an explanation. It is a purely verbal matter, he says – one might well say "two hundred and twenty-four to six" but not "two hundred and fourteen to six". But I think it just as likely that it would be quoted as "two one four to six", which seems to me perfectly permissible. In any case, I maintain that indexes are meant to be read and consulted rather than read aloud and in my own products I shall continue to defy the taboo – see the index to the present work – nor am I alone in this practice. Mr Rees also deprecates the giving of dates in the form "1792–801", which to me seems as harmless as "146–51".

Some indexers dispose of a sequence of references by the use of one of the following abbreviations after the initial reference number: f., ff., *et seq.* (=*et sequens*), *et seqq.* (or *sqq.*). Thus "8 f." and "8 *et seq.*" are supposed to denote "8 and the page following". Similarly, "23 ff." and "*et seqq.*" supposedly represent "and the pages following". This practice is to be deprecated, as lacking precision. It is far better to write "8–9" where the subject matter is referred to continuously on those pages in the text, and "8, 9" when other matter intervenes. Again, "23 ff." gives the user not the slightest indication how many pages are involved (whether two or twenty).

There exists, however, a useful device for indicating that the item is not referred to continuously; this can be done by inserting the word *passim* (Latin for "here and there") after the last numeral of the sequence group. Thus, "146–53 *passim*" indicates that the subject matter of the heading is referred to in *scattered passages throughout* those pages of the text. It can be seen at a glance that index space is often saved through such elimination of the intervening reference numbers (in this case, 147, 148, 149, 150, 151, 152).

For some reason (which is left unexplained) the use of *passim* for this purpose did not meet with the approval of the compilers of the 1964 British Standard on the preparation of indexes (BS 3700: 1964, para. 4.3.1) or that of the compilers of its successor (BS 3700: 1976, para. 5.3.1). I certainly consider, however, that the use of the term is fully justified, provided that only isolated mentions of the item are made in consecutive pages of the text. But I cannot think that the following index entry in an ornithological book was justified:

Birds, 1–457 *passim*

when 457 was the total number of pages in the text. The entry had been inserted at the proof stage by the indexer's young daughter and was not discovered until after the volume had appeared in print. It then caused so much amusement that the publisher decided to retain it in one or two subsequent editions.

When an indexer employs *passim*, its use should be noted and briefly explained in the preliminary note with which every well-constituted index of substance should start.

How many references in a row?

Wheatley remarked that "few things are more annoying than a long string of references without any indication of the cause of reference".[1] He was alluding to one of the cardinal vices of the untutored indexer – a vice that persists to this day. Sometimes one encounters a heading (particularly a proper-name heading) followed by a solid block of fifty or more unbroken references. Nothing could be more futile or more infuriating to the would-be user.

[1] *How to Make an Index*, p. 153.

Experiment has ascertained that the average time taken in tracing a reference to its source in the text is three-quarters of a minute. If, therefore, it was the fiftieth reference that pointed to the page with the required information, the search might take well over half an hour. Rather than waste all that time it is likely that the user would try skimming through the book's pages in the hope of lighting upon his quest.

It is generally accepted that the number of unbroken references after a heading or subheading should not exceed five (or at the most, seven, and then rarely). Oddly enough, an offender in this respect is the otherwise impeccable index to the already-quoted *Information Indexing* by John Metcalfe, where often as many as seventeen or eighteen unbroken references can be found strung together.

An exception is to be found in the author indexes to scientific books, where the references to each author's name are as many as the allusions to his works in the text. Another exception may be noted. When a heading is followed by a number of references pointing to aspects that are indexable but of no particular importance (that is to say, those in which a separate subheading would convey as much information as could be gathered from the text), these may be lumped together in a sub-entry (which should come last) with the subheading having some such wording as: "alluded to" (favoured by Wheatley) or "also mentioned" or "other references". In theory the number of these can be unlimited, but in practice it should not be excessive, for the reasons given above.

How can an excessive quantity of continuous reference numbers be curbed? The remedy is normally quite simple. In the case of a heading, the more important of its aspects indicated by the references can be transformed into subheadings, with an "alluded to" subheading at the end for the more trivial items:

Not

Legislative Assembly, 91, 100, 135, 147, 174, 175, 207, 215, 303, 321, 408, 426, 466, 481

but

Legislative Assembly:
  bomb explosions in (1929), 135
  Congress members resign from (1930), 147
  Congress success in elections for (1934), 207
  Congress "walk-out" from (1931), 174

elections for (1945), 303
"façade for Viceroy's rule"
(1919–47), 466
Government of India Act (1935)
and, 215
Nehru reports on riots to (1946),
321
Swarajist strength in (1923), 91,
100
alluded to, 175, 408, 426, 481

If it is a sub-entry itself that errs with excessive references, then the remedy is to turn it into a cross-reference to a separate heading having its own sub-entries. Thus:

Not
  Tutankhamen
    as Biphuria, 111, 275
    as Nebkheprure, 26, 62, 84, 90,
      111, 136, 173, 175, 176, 183,
      190, 195, 210, 236, 274, 275

but
  Biphuria (Tutankhamen's alterna-
    tive name), 111, 275
  Nebkheprure (Tutankhamen's al-
    ternative name):
    confusion over name, 90, 111,
      136
    Coronation use of, 26, 62, 84,
      175
    god Amun and, 173, 176, 183,
      195
    "house of", 190
    "living god, lord of the two
      lands", 210
    "triumphing over the Nine
      Bows", 274
    alluded to, 236, 275
  Tutankhamen
    as Biphuria, 111, 275
    as Nebkheprure, *see* Nebkheprure

It will be noticed that in the "Biphuria" entries the page references are repeated. This is one of the exceptional cases where double entry is recommended (see p. 111).

Dividing up the text page

Out of respect for the user's time and patience it is essential that, when the text pages of a book or periodical are divided into two or more columns, each shall be separately indicated in the index.

This is done by inserting an *a* or a *b* (more rarely, *c*, *d*, etc.) immediately after the page number: 17*a*; 39*c*–41*b*. Where a page
reference number is left unadorned by any following letter, that
should denote that the entry item is covered continuously in both
or all the text columns. A brief explanation of the practice is called
for in the preliminary note of any index concerned.

Some years ago, through the courtesy of the Superintendent of
the British Museum Reading Room (Mr Richard Bancroft, then
Chairman of the Society of Indexers) I was able to inspect some of
the Museum's older indexes and was surprised to find that some
very fine specimens were produced as early as the sixteenth century.
Thus, Polydore Vergil in his 31-page index (in Latin) to the second
edition of his *Urbanitatis Angliae Historiae* (1555) not only gave a
page reference for each item but also actually indicated on which
line of that page the sought piece of information appeared. Alas,
the modern index-user cannot expect to be similarly pampered
today, or only very rarely. One such exception is the index to the
Oxford Dictionary of Quotations (2nd edn, 1953), which for ease of
reference is unrivalled. Here each reference shows the text's page
number, followed by the numerical position of the quotation on
that page, e.g. 163 : 15 indicates the fifteenth quotation on page 163.

The user can be helped on occasion by the use of the Latin
words *bis* and *ter* after page references. It sometimes happens that
an item is alluded to in two or more quite unconnected passages
on the same page; a simple reference (say 172) in the index will
direct the user to that page where he may find an allusion near the
top, but, this not being what he is seeking, he may conclude
that it is not there, when all the time it was waiting for him in
a second allusion lower down. In such a case, by employing 172 *bis*
(="twice") or 172 *ter* (="thrice") or even 172 *quater* (="four
times") the indexer can provide adequate warning and prevent
the catastrophe.

Some indexers object to using *bis* and *ter*, which they charac-
terize as unnecessary spoon-feeding of the user; it is his business,
they maintain, to read in its entirety any page to which he may be
directed in the index. But such a contention makes no allowance
for the pace at which life is perforce lived today or for human
nature. In any event the practice (of using *bis* and *ter*) meets with
the approval of the British Standard, while I for one feel that any
device is well worth while whereby the path of people who consult

indexes is made smoother with a minimum of extra labour for the indexer.

Whenever *bis* and *ter* are used in an index, they must be briefly explained in its preliminary note.

Instead of *bis* and *ter*, some indexers like to put numbers in parentheses immediately after the page references: 23(2), 17(3).

References extraordinary

When an indexable item occurs in a footnote,[1] the reference number should be followed by a small "n." and, if necessary, this can have after it in parentheses the number of the note. The "n." should be close to the preceding figure: 18n., 21n.(4), 683n.(57). There is no need to give a reference to a footnote if the same item is dealt with in the page above (*not*, e.g., "18 & n.").

The reference number to an illustration or its caption or to a map or plan in the text can be shown in various ways. The indexer may insert "(illus.)" after the reference number, or else (preferably) mark the reference to be in italics, of course explaining the practice in the index's preliminary note:

> Niagara Falls (between Ontario and New York State), 49, 53–61, 54 (illus.), facing 60 (illus.), 72
> *or*
> Niagara Falls, 49, 53–61, *54, facing 60*, 72

Sometimes, in the place of "(illus.)", one may use "54 (fig. 21)" or "facing 60 (Plate V)". The same result can be achieved by means of subheadings:

> Niagara Falls, 53–61
>   height of, 49
>   map of, 54
>   photo of, facing 60
>   volume of water, 72

Distinct typography is also useful for giving special emphasis to certain more important references. For this it is best to employ

---

[1] A footnote or endnote that merely supplies the documentary authority for some statement in the text rarely needs to be indexed. But if it has reading matter that amplifies the text it may very likely require indexing.

boldface type, obtained in the manuscript by a *wavy* underline (～～～), accompanied by "bold" in the margin. Experience leads to the restriction of the use of boldface references to those occasions when the topic of the heading is referred to throughout a whole chapter or other complete *headlined* section.

Appeasement, 89, **120–33**, 158

The British Standard suggests, as an alternative, that the references for which emphasis is sought can be given priority in order. But that method seems to me clumsier and less precise.

Any typographical variant in the index must be explained in its preliminary note.

CROSS-REFERENCES

The first thing to note about a cross-reference is its form – complete with hyphen. In a previous work on indexing with which I was connected the publisher's editor enraged me by insisting on eliminating that hyphen, both in text and index. Now that last sentence is a cross reference, but it certainly does not constitute a cross-reference.

A cross-reference, unlike an ordinary reference, does not indicate the part of the text where the sought information conveyed by a heading or subheading may be found, but on the contrary points away to some other entry in the index. Since no index-user likes to be pushed around overmuch from entry to entry, cross-references should be limited in number to what are strictly needed. At the same time, there are numerous occasions on which they are vitally necessary for the proper functioning of an index, as has been shown in earlier chapters.

Writers on indexing have hitherto assumed that there are only two classes of cross-reference. I claim, however, that there are five distinct types:

See
See also
See under
See also under
q.v.

All of them are almost invariably printed in italics (and should accordingly be underlined in the manuscript "copy"). But in the case of the first four (that is, excluding "q.v.") they are better if distinguished by being printed in ordinary Roman type when it happens that they are immediately preceded by, as well as immediately followed by, words or expressions already rightfully in italics, e.g. foreign words, titles of publications, names of ships, etc.

> Furze, *see* Gorse
> *Morning Post, The* (see also *Daily Telegraph*)

"See" cross-references

A "see" cross-reference (sometimes called a "rejected heading") is defined in the British Standard as "a direction from one heading, after which there are no page or other references, to any other heading(s) under which relevant references are collected". That explains the term pretty well, but would have been more complete had the words "or subheading" been inserted after "a direction from one heading".

The most usual occasions on which a "see" cross-reference is called for are the following:

1) To refer from one synonym or "near-synonym" to another, whether the former occurs in the text or is merely introduced in the index because it is likely to be looked for by the user.

2) To merge antonyms in one entry.

3) In cases of inverted proper names, where either form is likely to be sought by the reader:

> Van Eyck, Hubert and Jan, *see* Eyck

4) For pseudonyms and married names:

> Twain, Mark, *see* Clemens, Samuel
> Burton, Mrs Richard, *see* Taylor, Elizabeth

(In both cases the reverse procedure is legitimate. The number of allusions to each in the text should decide the point.)

5) From generic to more specific terms:

> Tobacco, *see* Cigarette tobacco *and* Pipe tobacco

(This cross-reference implies that "Tobacco" in its overall sense is not dealt with in the text. All such cross-references should as far as possible be always in a *downward* direction, that is, from the general to the particular, the specific item forming the heading of the actual entry.)

6) From a shortened or popular term to the full or official or scientific form:

> Baking soda, *see* Sodium bicarbonate
> Christian Science, *see* Church of Christ, Scientist
> Coleridge's "Ancient Mariner", *see* "Rime of the Ancient Mariner, The"
> White ants, *see* Termites

(It is not suggested that the chosen headings are necessarily more correct than the rejected ones; they are shown simply as samples of what are likely to occur.)

7) In order to turn sub-entries into headings with their own subheadings (see p. 106).

Note the italicized "*and*" in example (5) above. This is important because with an ordinary Roman "and" it might be assumed that the cross-reference points to only one heading, "Cigarette tobacco and pipe tobacco". For the same reason, where the cross-reference is to more than two headings, they must be separated by semicolons, never by commas:

> Schools, *see* Approved schools; Comprehensive schools *and* Grammar schools

For ease of reference "see" cross-references can and should be avoided by repeating the references whenever there are not more than, say, three of them and there are no sub-entries. That is the method of double (or even triple or quadruple) entry, not otherwise to be recommended. The number of references is limited so as to preclude taking up an extra line. Thus, take the case of allusions in the text to "the electronic indexing of the Dead Sea Scrolls". Here conceivably the following three index entries are indicated:

> Dead Sea Scrolls, electronic indexing of, 13, 97, 105
> Electronic indexing of Dead Sea Scrolls, 13, 97, 105
> Indexing of Dead Sea Scrolls, electronic, 13, 97, 105

The only danger is that in the absence of cross-references the indexer may forget, when he comes to the second allusion to the matter in the text, that the fresh reference number must be added to all the other entries. This risk of incomplete entries can be eliminated if he pencils at the top of each card or slip the other headings affected.

"See also" cross-references

A "see also" cross-reference does not constitute a "rejected heading" nor does it deny in any way the validity of the heading or subheading after which it is placed. On the contrary it merely points to some other heading(s) showing where additional relevant information can be obtained in the text.

The position of this cross-reference in an analytical entry is a matter of some importance and has been the subject of conflict. Some authorities maintain that it should come last in the entry, while others contend that it is best placed immediately after the heading or subheading to which it applies. The latter method is certainly to be preferred, for the very good reason that it saves the user's time by giving him early warning of what is *not* to be found (in the case of a heading) in what may be the numerous subheadings below. In this position it must be inserted in parentheses.

The most common use of "see also" cross-references is to call the researcher's attention to related headings, whether co-ordinate or subordinate. Thus, the cumulated index to *Chemical Abstracts* (1937–46) contains the following:

> Particles (*see also* Absorbed substances; Brownian movement; Colloids; Dilitancy; Dispersion; Drops; Dust; Electrophoresis; Lyosorption; Micelles; Photophoresis; Radiation; Sedimentation; Separation; Suspensions: Tactoids) . . .
> Photoelectric effect (*see also* Hall effect; Shenstone effect) . . .

"See under" and "see also under"

These offsprings have precisely the characteristics of their respective parents save in one particular: they do not actually refer to the named heading but to its subheading or one of its subheadings. It is this distinction that entitles them to rank as separate types of cross-reference:

> *Snow White and the Seven Dwarfs, see under* Disney, Walter

At this stage it is necessary to utter a word of warning, which applies to all the four forms of cross-reference so far treated (but not to "q.v.", which follows). Several writers on indexing (particularly in America) insist that the heading pointed to in a cross-reference shall be quoted in full, punctuation and all, exactly as it stands as part of an entry. Such a practice can involve a prodigious waste of time for the indexer and a prodigious waste of space in the index, especially if the cross-references are very plentiful and the referenced headings are elaborate. For instance, is it really necessary to use such a cumbrous cross-reference as "*see also* Unesco (United Nations Educational, Scientific and Cultural Organization)", supposing that the main heading (as is likely) appears in that form? Would not "*see also* Unesco" suffice?

British practice, I consider, requires only the repetition of the keyword together (if necessary) with just enough following words to render the referenced heading readily identifiable beyond a peradventure. Naturally in an index containing such consecutive headings, shall we say, as:

Health, drinking a
Health, Ministry of
Health and happiness

a cross-reference like "Ministry of Health, *see* Health" simply would not do, and it would be necessary to use the complete inverted form.

"*q.v.*"

The expression "q.v." stands for the Latin *quod vide* ("which see"). As a cross-reference it has this peculiarity that, although like the other forms it refers *to* a heading, it does not, unlike them, refer *from* a heading or subheading; instead it applies only to a single word or expression therein, indicating that that word or expression can itself be turned to as a heading in the same index. It always immediately follows that word or expression, is put in italics and usually (but not necessarily) in parentheses:

> Sixtieth Rifles (King's Royal Rifle Corps, now the Greenjackets, *q.v.*), 197, 203
> Balfour, Arthur James, xxv, 285
> on the Jameson Raid (*q.v.*), 286

Nowadays "q.v." cross-references are not found very frequently in indexes, but in their proper context and within their own limitations they can serve a useful purpose as a space-saving device.

"Blind" cross-references

My readers need scarcely be reminded that, whichever of the foregoing five types of cross-reference is used, it is essential to ensure that the heading (or subheading) to which attention is directed does actually exist in the index. Wheatley cites an instance from Eadie's *Dictionary of the Bible* (1850): "Dorcas *see* Tabitha", but there is no entry under Tabitha at all. The moral? Verify your cross-references.

Nothing infuriates a would-be seeker after knowledge more than to be confronted with one of such blind cross-references, unless it be to find himself led on a "wild goose chase" (as G. V. Carey termed it) involving a whole series of them, e.g.:

> Advertising, *see* Posters
> Posters, *see* Publicity
> Publicity, *see* Advertising

Examples of blind cross-references are still to be encountered from time to time in printed indexes. They are due to careless editing by the indexer (or the publisher's editor) – except in the rare cases where a whole entry has been omitted by the printer, and the proof-reader(s) have overlooked the omission.

CHAPTER SEVEN
Alphabetical Arrangement

The Index is a great leveller.
attributed to Bernard Shaw (1856–1950)

Although, despite diligent research, I have not been able to trace the exact source of the above quotation (whether play, preface or other writing), George Bernard Shaw is clearly referring to the Vatican's *Index Librorum Prohibitorum* (list of prohibited books), which placed his name in the company of Moreau, Wilde and Zola. But, thanks to alphabetical arrangement, it is just as applicable to most book and periodical indexes, and it must have been the cause of much chagrin to Shaw to find in so many of them his name appearing in the closest proximity to that of Shakespeare but always *after* that of the other playwright.

But I must return to the subject of this chapter, which is alphabetical arrangement, not authorship of quotations. It is not absolutely essential for an index to be arranged alphabetically and, as we shall see, even in one normally so arranged it may prove more convenient to have certain parts arranged in some numerical, chronological or other non-alphabetical order. Moreover, as John Metcalfe has pointed out,[1] familiarity with the order of the alphabet beyond one or two letters is not so widespread as is commonly supposed. Even the more erudite are vague about it and do not realize its exact use in indexing, that is the use of as many letters as are necessary to distinguish separate headings and subheadings.

All that can be done about that state of affairs is to pray for a wider and more complete level of education. For while it may be true that alphabetic writing is recognized as one of the great

---

[1] *Alphabetical Subject Indication of Information* (1965), p. 147.

promoters and aids of civilization, alphabetic indexing is not, yet the latter has certainly come to stay and has virtually no rival in the indexing of books and periodicals.

The British Standards

The subject of alphabetical arrangement deserves and has its own British Standard, BS 1749: or rather there are two, because BS 1749: 1951, *Alphabetical Arrangement*, contained some rules that proved distasteful to the computer when it tried its hand on compiling indexes, and so it was considerably revised in the more recent BS 1749: 1969, *Specification for Alphabetical Arrangement and the Filing Order of Numerals and Symbols*.

There is also some valuable information about alphabetical arrangement in BS 3700: 1976, *Recommendations [for] the preparation of indexes*, which I shall quote in its place. Later in this chapter I shall have something to say about the computer-compiled London telephone directory.

However, as we are not all computer programmers but rather operative or manual indexers, I do not think that we need necessarily feel bound by the new rules and I therefore propose to quote both sets (BS 1749 of 1951 *and* 1969), where they differ, leaving it to the individual reader to choose which he prefers to follow, so long as he is mindful that any particular practice which he picks must be adhered to rigidly throughout any one index.

First of all, the older Standard (of 1951) seems to contemplate the existence of only one index, and that an alphabetical one. The Standard of 1969, on the other hand, prescribes that the alphabetical index shall, when necessary, be preceded by *two* others, the first of symbols, the second of numerals. But, as the need to use either symbols or numerals as keywords is very seldom encountered, we will defer their discussion until later. All that need be said here is that, supposing there is only one symbol or one numeral to be treated under the new rule, it would seem very lonely standing there is solitary state! We will come at once to alphabetical arrangement, which is, after all, the subject of this chapter.

Single-word headings and identical keywords

The arrangement of single-word headings should present no difficulty. But both Standards think it worth while stating explicitly (what one would have imagined to be mere ordinary common sense) that where one word differs from another only by the presence of additional letters at the end, the shorter word shall come first (e.g. Fellows before Fellowship).

Where several headings have an identical keyword, the single-word heading will come first, and an inverted heading must precede one with no comma separating the keyword from the following word or words:

Oxford, 53–78
Oxford, Robert Harley, 1st Earl of (1661–1724), 92
Oxford and Asquith, 1st Earl of (1852–1928), 115
Oxford Union Society, the, 65–6

In such instances it is greatly preferable to repeat the keyword on each occasion rather than employ the often futile (and sometimes dangerous) line known as a rule, or dash:

Oxford, . . .
————, Robert . . .
———— and Asquith . . .

And as for "————shire" . . . , need anything be said about this horror? In a list of identical surnames, as for instance in a telephone directory, their order should be determined by the inverted initials or forenames that follow them:

Collins, H.
Collins, H. J.
Collins, Harold
Collins, Henry John
Collins, Hugh

But in the alphabetical arrangement of their latest telephone directories the British postal authorities have seen fit to flout the conventional rules of indexing.

By their new method, introduced in the summer of 1970, only the initial letters of subscribers' first forenames are used in deciding the order in which they are listed. So Hugh Collins,

Harold Collins and H. Collins are all lumped together with the other H. Collinses, their precise order depending upon the alphabetical arrangement of the ensuing road, street, avenue or equivalent address. Thus:

Collins, Hugh, 91 Chancery Lane
Collins, Harold, 128 Fleet Street
Collins, H., 85 The Strand
Collins, Henry John, 133 Cheapside
Collins, H. J., 47 Regent Street.

The new system evoked a storm of protest from customers who were well satisfied with the old arrangement. Possibly made as a change for change's sake, or more probably to pander to computer economy, it does not appear to give any additional ease of reference to the harassed hunter of telephone numbers in a directory.

Homonyms

Homonyms, as we saw in Chapter 4, are two or more words or expressions having the same form but different meanings. Such words or expressions must invariably be made separate headings, otherwise we shall find ourselves committing such flagrant errors as the following (both from actual indexes):

Mill on Liberty
———— *the Floss, The*
Lamb and Coleridge
———————— mint sauce

Both the British Standard on indexing (BS 3700: 1976) and the American Standard Basic Criteria are agreed on the order in which homonyms should be indexed:

Order	*Examples*
1. Person or organization	London, Jack (novelist)
2. Place	London (England)
3. Subject	London, population of
4. Title of publication	*London, History of*

The order for personal homonyms is for forenames (with titles or appellations only) to precede surnames. The former may be arranged either in alphabetical order of titles or appellations or in hierarchical order:

Alphabetical	*Hierarchical*
John, Archduke	John, Saint
John, Count	John, Pope
John, Emperor	John, Emperor
John, King	John, King
John, Pope	John, Archduke
John, Saint	John, Count
John, Augustus	John, Sir William
John, Sir William	John, Augustus

Geographic homonyms, I suggest, had best be indexed in gazetteer order, that is:

1) Cities and towns (with region and/or country in parentheses)
2) Administrative areas (county, province, state, etc.)
3) Physical feature appellations (Bay, Cape, Island, Lake, River, etc.—the appellations often abbreviated)

The homonyms in each of the above parts should be arranged according to the alphabetical order of the words following them:

Alexandria (Dunbarton, Scotland)
Alexandria (Egypt)
Alexandria (Rumania)
Alexandria, *isle* (Antarctic)
Alexandria, *lake* (Ontario, Canada)
Alexandria Bay, *city* (NY, USA)
Alexandria Station (N. Territory, Australia)

Subject homonyms (other than proper names) are differentiated by qualifying expressions and arranged in alphabetical order accordingly:

Pipes (conduit)
Pipes (music)
Pipes (smoking)

It should be noted that the heading must be repeated for each homonym.

When titles of works or publications are identical, they are differentiated by adding the name of the author or sponsor, or in the case of newspapers or periodicals, the name of the place of publication:

> *Old Wives' Tale* (Arnold Bennett – novel)
> *Old Wives' Tale* (Heywood – play)
>
> *Natura* (Amsterdam)
> *Natura* (Bucharest)
> *Natura* (Milan)

Simple abbreviations

By "simple" is meant an abbreviation of a single word, as opposed to compound abbreviations, which will be treated later. When it consists of a single letter of the word, it naturally comes at the beginning of that letter in the index, others following in strict alphabetical order, just as spelled:

> C., *see* Carbon
> Ca., *see* Calcium
> Calcium
> Carbon
> Chlorine
> Cl., *see* Chlorine
> Copper
> Cu., *see* Copper

Other simple abbreviations are also alphabetized exactly as spelt, but with two exceptions – the "Mac" names and those beginning with the contracted word "St".

Names that start with Mc or M' are treated in British indexes as though those prefixes were spelt *Mac* (of which they are both contractions), the order in each case being determined by the letter or letters that follow:

> "Mac" names
> Macaque monkeys
> MacArthur, Gen. Douglas
> M'Carthy, Justin Huntley
> McCarthy, Lillah
> Macgillicuddy's Reeks
> Machine Gun Corps
> Macmillan, Rt Hon. Harold

This rule is not always followed in the United States, where some indexes (especially computer-compiled ones) and some telephone directories alphabetize M' and Mc just as spelt. Also it should be noted that with African names the prefix M' is not a contraction for Mac. Thus the township of M'Baiki would have to be listed between, say, Mazgirt (Turkey) and Mbala.

Similarly the abbreviation *St* as part of a name is treated as if spelt out in full – Saint:

St Abb's Head (Berwickshire)
St Albans, 12th Duke of
St Bartholomew's Hospital
Saint Joan (Bernard Shaw)
St Johnston, Sir Reginald
St Moritz
Saint-Pierre, Bernardin de
Saints, The, Battle of (1782)

The position of St Moritz in the above list should be noted. Strictly it is not accurately placed here, as its "St" stands not for Saint but for Sankt. It is thought, however, that the vast majority of index-users would be likely to look for it in this place rather than after "Saints".

Compound headings

These, whether hyphened or not, should be indexed under the initial letter of the first element (see pp. 68–70, with the exceptions stated on pp. 70–1 and 85–6).

But in their relation both to one another and to single-word headings, compound headings can be alphabetized in two distinct ways, each of which is in fairly general use. This has long led to fierce controversy between the adherents of the rival systems and given rise to what in the realm of alphabetical arrangement I may call the "Great Divide": that between the Word-by-word and the Letter-by-letter systems.

Word-by-word and letter-by-letter systems

A compound heading can be indexed either as a group of separate words each alphabetized in turn – the Word-by-word method (New York before Newark) – or it can be treated as a single entity, alphabetized all through – the Letter-by-letter method (Newark

before New York). Let us take some examples of each system, so
as to be able to compare them:

Word-by-word	*Letter-by-letter*
South, Robert	South, Robert
South African cricketers	South African cricketers
South Australia	Southampton
South Carolina	South Australia
Southampton	Southborough (Kent)
Southborough	South Carolina
Southcott, Joanna	Southcott, Joanna
Southend-on-Sea	Southend-on-Sea

Although there may not seem a vast difference in the order of
those two lists, yet it can be imagined how widely separated some
of the words affected would become in a long index.

BS 1749: 1951 (*Alphabetical Arrangement*) whole-heartedly backed
the word-by-word system. BS 3700: 1964 (*Recommendations for the
Preparation of Indexes*)[1] took a more neutral attitude, pointing out
that the letter-by-letter system (which it placed first) has the
advantage that a given compound always occupies the same
position, whether shown as two or more separate words (e.g.
Water glass), or as a hyphened compound (Water-glass) or as a
single word (Waterglass); on the other hand, a word-by-word
arrangement sometimes results in a clearer grouping of related
words, bringing, for instance, Water, Water-mills and Water-
wheels in close proximity, whereas by the letter-by-letter method
they would be interrupted by, shall we say, Waterford and Water-
proofing.

The later Standard on alphabetical arrangement (BS 1749: 1969)
plumped for word-by-word, going so far as to state that the other
system is "not recommended". This is surely too sweeping. While
the letter-by-letter system is virtually unknown in Britain as
far as the indexing of histories, biographies, religious and philo-
sophical treatises and belles-lettres is concerned, yet it certainly has
its uses in encyclopaedias (in both text and index), in the indexes
to atlases and gazetteers and in those to certain scientific and
technological works. Indeed, the only encyclopaedia that I can
recall as having employed a word-by-word arrangement for its
articles and index is the *Encyclopaedia Americana*.

[1] The recommendations of the new British Standard on indexes, BS 3700: 1976,
on this point do not differ significantly.

Both systems have their anomalies; both have their devoted adherents among indexers. The word-by-word method may require cross-references when a keyword has plausible solid, hyphened and two-word forms, as with "Waterglass" above, but any such cross-references should be deleted when they are found to adjoin the principal entry.

The word-by-word method has its disadvantages. As Mr Neil Fisk, a staunch advocate of the letter-by-letter method, has pointed out,[1] "everybody would expect 'Shipbreakers' to come before 'Shipbrokers' ": but in *U.K. Kompass* (a register of the products and services provided by the whole of British manufacturing industry and commerce, with 27,000 headings in its index), " 'Ship brokers' is *followed* by 'Shipbreakers'. . . and they are almost four inches apart with 36 other entries between them, including those for 'Ship models', and 'Ship test tanks' preceding 'Ships' bells'. This is because the first compound, with 'brokers', appears as two words and the second, with 'breakers', as one, and the indexing is word by word."

But the letter-by-letter method also requires an important exception. The University of Chicago Press prefers that system of alphabetizing and any index prepared for a Chicago book must be so arranged. But the Chicago *Manual of Style*, 12th edn (1969), asserted quite definitely that in this mode "one carries it all through the heading; that is, one ignores spaces and commas[2] between words and alphabetizes headings as if they were single words". Mr J. Arthur Greenwood points out[3] that the wording quoted would justify the submission of an index containing the sequence:

Clarke, Edwin
Clarke, Jeremiah
Clark, Eugene

[1] *The Indexer*, Vol. 6, No. 2 (Autumn 1968), p. 44.
[2] But see "South, Robert" in the examples on p. 122. Also, in the indexes to atlases and gazetteers which use the letter-by-letter method a comma between two words normally breaks the sequence:
    Burton (Cheshire)
    Burton (Cumbria)
    Burton, North (Humberside)
    Burton Agnes (Humberside)
    Burton Bradstock (Dorset)
[3] *The Indexer*, Vol. 7, No. 1 (Spring 1970), p. 24.

He suggests, therefore, that the following exception must be made: "in indexing personal names, the family name governs the alphabetization, and the Christian name is used only to break ties".

It is true that the *Manual* does allow for two exceptions to the rigorous application of the letter-by-letter system. One is the handling of Mac names and the other the alphabetizing of subheadings that start with unimportant words (e.g. *and, as, at, for, in, of, to*). To take an example from the book's own index:

> Punctuation
>   with appositives
>   of classical references
>   correcting, in proofs
>   in direct quotations

But I suggest that it would be far better to eliminate all these false keywords ("with", "of", "in"), and this can easily be done in one of three ways: (a) by substituting the noun's possessive case (appositives', classical references', direct quotations'); (b) by altering the wording of the subheading so as to bring the actual keyword to the front ("appositives sometimes require"); or, if the worst comes to the worst, (c) by transposing the offending conjunction or preposition to the end, following a comma ("appositives, with"). This method applies particularly to legal indexing.

Unless given special instructions by the publisher, the indexer must decide before undertaking his task which method he proposes to use and should declare it in his preliminary note. He will probably choose according to the class of book, as I have indicated above, or else according to the mode to which he is the more accustomed. Whichever he selects, he must conform to it consistently throughout his index. If he is indexing an encyclopaedia or other work in which the contents are arranged in alphabetical order, he must use the same style as the text.

Compound abbreviations and acronyms

These, unlike the simple abbreviations, are affected by the choice between word-by-word and letter-by-letter. They consist of one or more abbreviated words (such as *nem. con.*) or else of a set of initial letters (such as M.A./MA, or B.B.C./BBC). Often the latter are written as one word (such as UNESCO or Aslib), in which case they are called acronyms, and should be indexed as one word under either system. Otherwise, under the old word-by-word rule, each letter of the set of initials counts as a separate word and all such sets come (in alphabetical sequence) at the beginning of the particular letter. But the revised alphabetical arrangement Standard (BS 1749: 1969) lays down that all such sets of abbreviations shall be treated as one word, unless the separation of the individual elements is indicated by spaces. In other words, for the sake of the computer's convenience, it has in this instance reverted to the letter-by-letter arrangement, which is (otherwise) "not recommended". But I do not consider that the manual indexer need feel bound by this ruling; if he prefers, he can still use the order of the examples on the left in the following table:

Word-by-word		*Letter-by-letter*
M.A.E.E.	Marine Aircraft Experimental Establishment	M.A.E.E.
		MAGGI
M/C	Marginal Credit	Maser
M.G.M.	Metro-Goldwyn-Meyer	M/C
M.I.D.A.S.	Measurement Information and Data Analysis System	MEDLARS
		M.G.M.
M.I.T.	Massachusetts Institute of Technology	MIDAS
		M.I.D.A.S.
MAGGI	Million Ampere Generator	M.I.T.
Maser	Microwave amplification by stimulated emission of radiation	
MEDLARS	Medical Literature Analysis and Retrieval System	
MIDAS	Missile Defence Alarm System	

An example of a compound expression whose elements are separated by spaces would be: *Jap. J. App. Phys.* (*Japanese Journal of Applied Physics*).

The new British Standard on indexes (BS 3700: 1976) permits abbreviations in the form of initial letters "representing a proper name" to be alphabetized by either method. Thus "NSW", it says, can be alphabetized either as a single word following "New" or as three words preceding "New". Nowadays, when full points are frequently omitted from such abbreviations, it is apparently of no consequence that the three "words" forming "NSW" are not separated from one another in any way.

Hyphened compounds

The old rule, with plenty of common sense to recommend it, was that under the word-by-word system the parts separated by hyphens counted as separate words unless one element was a prefix (or suffix) that was unable to stand alone in that sense. Examples of such prefixes are:

ante- anti- non- post- pre- pro- pseudo-

But the revisers of the Standard on alphabetical arrangement have seen fit to remove the exception (for the computer's convenience), so that now, if the manual indexer cares to follow the new rule, he will have to count "non-belligerent", "pre-Raphaelite" and "stand-in" in each case as two separate words:

non-belligerent
non-intervention
nonage

Pre-Raphaelite
preach

stand-in
standardization

The new Standard on indexes, on the other hand, takes the opposite view, recommending the letter-by-letter method, "since affixes will not be sought as words on their own". This seems to restore the rule of common sense – and, when doctors disagree, the indexer may feel justified in deciding the matter for himself.

Apostrophes

The apostrophe marking a possessive case is treated in a similar way by the new Standard on alphabetical arrangement, which lays down that it must henceforth count as a space for filing purposes. This means that instead of the order as at present, for instance, in the London telephone directory:

Partridge, Stanley
Partridge, W. W. D.
Partridge-King, F. E.
Partridge's

we shall, if we agree, have to use something like this:

Partridge, K. A.
Partridge-King, F. E.
Partridge, Leslie
Partridge's
Partridge, Stanley

Whether the telephone directory authorities will be willing to mend their ways accordingly I am unable to say. As the books are now, I believe, compiled by a computer, I should have thought they would already have done so, if they were going to make any change. Personally I hope they will not.

So much for the possessive apostrophe-s. The new Standard on alphabetical arrangement does not deal with another form of apostrophe, that marking an elision, as in:

"It's a long way to Tipperary"
It's Never Too Late to Mend

But as it states that the above rule does not apply to cases of transliteration where an apostrophe represents a letter, we may take it, I think, that it does not apply to the apostrophe in "It's", which will accordingly be allowed to count as one word.

The revised Standard on indexes, once again, differs from the revised Standard on alphabetical arrangement, declaring that "the apostrophe should be disregarded and the word in which it occurs treated as one word".

Accents and diacritical marks

These do not affect the alphabetical order of the words they adorn, except that in the case of two words spelt with the same letters, one word containing an accent or diacritical mark, and the other without, the latter should be placed first.

Some examples (the geographical names are extracted from the *Oxford Atlas* index) are:

ales and stouts
Ales (France)
Alesund (Norway)
Alvsborg (Swedish county)

Aruaña (Brazil)
Aš (Czechoslovakia)
'Ashar (Iraq)
Åswān (Egypt)

Both the German umlaut ö and the Danish letter ø are treated as
o and not as oe. Thus, Marshal von Göring, if spelt that way in the
text, should be listed in the index after "Gorilla". But there should
be a cross-reference from "Goering".

None the less, the complete disregard of modified words can be
risky in any index that is likely to be used internationally. Thus, a
German whose typewriter does not include ä, ö and ü may write
these letters as ae, oe, ue (unless he types "a" etc. and then adds
the umlaut by hand), and this practice would affect the alphabetical
indexing order, e.g. of words like Öl (Oel). As a rule Americans
also follow that method. On the other hand, Scandinavians place
words beginning with "ae" and "ø" after "z" in the alphabetical
order, as also do the Danes with words starting with "å". Again,
there is the Polish "Ł", which is a different letter from the ordinary
"l". Cross-references provide the only good answer to most of
these problems.

Symbols and numerals

It is not easy to imagine circumstances in which a symbol may have
to be used as the keyword of a heading, but it might well come as
the second word and so affect the order where there are several
headings with the same keyword. The original British Standard on
indexes (BS 3700: 1964) recommended that symbols be arranged
as if spelt out:

= as if "equals"
$ as if "dollars"
− as if "minus"
+ as if "plus"
% as if "per cent"
£ as if "pounds"

The revised Standard on alphabetical arrangement (BS 1749: 1969)
goes further and suggests that they be actually spelt out. It gives
further examples:

$x^2 + y^2$ spell out as "x squared plus y squared"
x-rays   spell out as "alpha-rays"

But for the life of me I cannot see why "x-rays" cannot be inserted as it stands under X, where most people are likely to look. BS 3700: 1976 takes a middle course, recommending that symbols be arranged in sequence preceding the alphabetical sequence, unless they are few in number, when they may be arranged as if spelt out.

The ampersand (&) can usually be spelt out as "and", but in the unlikely event of its occurring as the keyword it must be spelled out as "ampersand". Where it occurs inside a heading, it can be ignored for the purposes of filing order, as is done in the London telephone directories:

Debenham, Clive
Debenham & Co., solicitors
Debenham, Frederick

This treatment would appear to be authorized by BS 3700: 1976, which expressly allows "connecting articles, conjunctions and prepositions in names . . . or in titles beginning with the same word" to be "ignored in alphabetization to obtain a single A–Z array of subsequent significant words". It suggests, however, that those suppressed words should be parenthesized or else subordinated in some way typographically. Examples:

Journal (of The) Institute of Fuel
Journal (of) Pharmacy

Society (of) Indexers
Society (for) Psychical Research

The telephone directories do not, however, indulge in these suppressing tactics, but treat "of" and "for" as words that count:

Society for Psychical Research
Society of Analytical Research

As already stated, BS 1749: 1969 suggests separate indexes for both symbols and numerals, to precede the ordinary alphabetical one.[1] But this seems to me mere proliferation of indexes, to the hindrance of ease of reference. Far better to spell out the numerals (or at any rate to arrange them as if spelt out), and then insert them in proper sequence in the alphabetical index:

4th Hussars	*i.e.*	Fourth Hussars
5th Avenue		Fifth Avenue
10 Downing St		Ten Downing Street
100		One hundred
1066		Ten sixty-six
1848		Eighteen forty-eight (or, if not a date,
		One thousand eight hundred and forty-eight)
but		
1001 Nights		*Thousand and one Nights, A*
20 ans après		*Vingt ans après*
100 Best Stories		*Hundred Best Stories*

Where a numeral marks one of a series, it would be folly to give it either an alphabetical appearance or an alphabetical order. Such items should be listed serially:

Henry II, King of England
Henry VIII, King of England
Henry II, King of France

Uranium 235
Uranium 236
Uranium 238

1,2,3-xylenol ⎫
1,2,5-xylenol ⎬ under X
1,3,4-xylenol ⎭

Not so long ago one heard of an American computer that was set to work to compile the index to an important historico-religious work. We are told that it "dug in its heels" against following such a numerical order as I have described, insisting upon a strictly alphabetical order. Unless, therefore, the machine has been "brought to heel" (to vary the metaphor), one can expect to find certain occupiers of the Holy See egregiously listed as follows:

Urban VIII, Pope
Urban V

[1] It actually prescribes *two* numerical indexes, not to be interfiled. The first is for roman numerals, the second for arabic numerals. BS 3700: 1976 makes the same recommendation.

Urban IV
Urban I
Urban VII
Urban VI
Urban III
Urban II

Similarly we should use a numerical order in subheadings, even when the numbers are actually spelt out in the text:

Society of Indexers, The
   First Annual Report
   Second Annual Report
   Fourth Annual Report

Where the numbers do *not* indicate a series, the items should be indexed in their normal order:

  100 Years War (under H)
    6 Days War (under S)
   30 Years War (under T)

Other non-alphabetical orders

It is sometimes expedient to desert alphabetical order in favour of some other arrangement, say a chronological or evolutionary or some varied order, so long as it is systematic. This is particularly true of subheadings:

Geological eras
   Paleozoic
   Mesozoic
   Tertiary
   Quaternary

Land routes
   Motorways: M1 . . .; M2 . . .
   Major A roads: A1 . . . etc.
   Minor B roads: B . . .
   Lanes and tracks . . .

As I explained in Chapter 3, a chronological order is also useful sometimes in the case of "run-on" subheadings in the index to a history or biography.

CHAPTER EIGHT
The Indexing of Periodicals

The indexing of periodicals is based on the same principles as those for the indexing of books, but it involves a stricter discipline, a wider knowledge and unswerving consistency.

Robert L. Collison, *Indexes and Indexing*

The Concise Oxford Dictionary defines a periodical as a magazine or miscellany "published at regular intervals, e.g. monthly". On the other hand, strictly a journal (derived from Latin *diurnus*) should mean a *daily* record of events (e.g. a diary or newspaper) but has come to be the equivalent of a periodical, often with the particular sense of the proceedings of some society or institution.

More than 90,000 periodicals in various countries are listed in the Unesco *Statistical Yearbook* (1976) and the addition of more obscure ones might bring the actual total in existence to considerably more. How many of the 90,000 have their own indexes it would be quite impossible to say; any wider conclusion drawn from a sample survey of 100 British commercially published periodicals which showed that 88 per cent contained indexes (of a sort) would be misleading.[1]

Categories of periodicals

The style of indexing required will depend to some extent on the type and readership of the periodical concerned. Virtually all periodicals are highly specialized, but those on sale to the general public are, in general, no more difficult to index, at least in terms of subject matter, than books on similar subjects. Other periodicals, such as those academic journals that publish original research or

[1] *The Indexer*, Vol. 7, No. 2 (Autumn 1970), pp. 70–9.

abstracts,[1] and some trade and professional journals, are too abstruse to be safely tackled by an indexer who does not have at least a fairly thorough grounding in the subject in question.

In recent years there has been a revival of interest in "part-work" publication, i.e. the issuing of biggish books in instalments at regular intervals, usually in magazine format. Although, with their fixed term of publication, part-works cannot properly be considered as magazines, they are undoubtedly published periodically and in appearance often closely resemble magazines.

Unfortunately, a far too high proportion of present-day periodicals of all kinds are published either without indexes or with inadequate ones. As Wheatley observed more than seventy years ago, "The indexes of some periodicals are good, but those of the many are bad."[2]

Differences from book indexing

The general principles of indexing, as enunciated in previous chapters, apply equally to books and periodicals. But the very nature of the latter necessitates some divergence both in procedure and technique (particularly in the form of the entries).

In the first place, whereas a book index can usually be tackled in one "go" (though not of course in one session), the periodical indexer, after completing his index to one number, will have to wait for the next weekly, monthly or quarterly issue, and this may result in some strain on the consistency of his subject headings. Further, he may be indexing not a single periodical but a number of separate ones (as, for example, is done in the *British Humanities Index*), all of which are available at the same time.

Secondly, most periodicals and serials contain a number of widely varied articles, each by a separate author, while a book is as a rule devoted to a single theme, with a logical connexion between successive chapters. But I fail to find any justification for the common practice of providing periodicals with an Author index

---

[1] *Chemical Abstracts* provides an outstanding example of a research aid wherein the indexes, to develop their full value, take up nearly two-thirds as much space as the text. Dr Holmstrom has declared that "so far from the indexing being merely an adjunct to the text it would be truer to regard the text of the Abstracts as expanded annotations of the necessarily brief indications of the original literature given in the form of index entries".

[2] *How to Make an Index*, p. 59.

as well as a Subject index in place of one general index, or of departing from Wheatley's principle of "the index one and indivisible" (with the exception, as noted earlier, of some scientific journals).

Thirdly, few books are nowadays printed with the text having more than one column, whereas periodicals very often have two, three or even sometimes four columns. In every such case the column in which the required item is to be found must be carefully distinguished, as explained in Chapter 6 (pp. 106–7). The practice should be briefly explained as one of the index's preliminary notes.

As regards the form of the index entry, headings and subheadings are chosen in much the same way as for monographs, except that the indexer must be exceedingly cautious about using either the full title of a periodical article or even a word or expression from that title as a heading – see pp. 89 and 137. Also what has been said about cross-references (Chapter 6) applies equally to periodicals and to books. It is in the matter of the references themselves that the chief difference can lie.

If the index is to *one* periodical, which is paginated consecutively throughout the indexable period, then there is no problem and the references will consist of simple page numbers, as in book indexing. (Paragraph numbers do not apply to journals and periodicals.) But if, as in the case of some periodicals, the pagination starts afresh with each issue, it is essential to pinpoint that issue; this can be done by inserting immediately before the reference the number of that particular issue, followed by a colon, or, where the index is an annual one to a monthly publication, by an abbreviated form of the month, perhaps in parentheses. Where a new series of the periodical is started every so often, it will be necessary to add the year of publication, as clearly there will be more than one issue bearing any particular number. Thus:

Drug addiction: curing the heroin addict (John Campbell), 70 (3 D 65), 366–8

(The abbreviations used for the dates should, of course, be explained, with other abbreviations, in the preliminary note.)

Should, however, the index be to a collection of abstracts, or to a review of a number of periodicals, more will be required, for now each entry must contain the title (perhaps abbreviated) of the particular journal(s) being quoted:

Birth control:
    Abortion in the Soviet Union, *Soviet Studies*, No. 17 (Jl 65), 76–83
    Catholics and, *New Statesman*, No. 69 (5 Mr 65), 345

Regular features

A further distinguishing mark of periodicals is that many of them, in addition to their original communications (that is, their ordinary articles), carry under the same title in each issue certain habitual features. Such are: Leading articles (or Leaders); Letters to the Editor; Book reviews; Obituaries. These can be indexed in classified form under those headings, provided that each theme or personal name in the subheadings is given also its own individual entry. Where the space allowed for the index will not permit such dual entries, it must be the classification schemes that are sacrificed.

As a sub-entry under the class heading "Leading articles" or "Editorials", each item can appear in quotes under its full title in the text, merely inverting an initial definite or indefinite article for the sake of the alphabetical arrangement:

Leaders
    "Are we to survive?", 91
    "Crocodile Tears", 57
    "Drama of the High Seas, A", 115
    "Involuntary environment", 173

But for the specific heading the use of the title as it stands should not be attempted, unless it precisely describes the main topic of the editorial (e.g. "The European Economic Community"), which certainly none of the above editorial titles do; this is because present-day editors and leader writers tend to prefer something rather more sprightly, that will catch the reader's attention. In such a case a fitting subject entry will have to be chosen, with if possible an indication of the editorial attitude as a modification:

European Economic Community, Prime Minister blamed for British entry
    (edl), 1–5

(There would, of course, have to be cross-references from "Common Market" if this term was used in the text. For the abbreviation "edl", see below.) One or two name headings may also be necessary for persons prominently alluded to in the editorial, especially if those persons are otherwise referred to in the index:

Heath, Edward (Prime Minister), 19, 21
   and European Economic Community (edl), 2–4

Letters to the Editor, if classified at all, appear under that heading simply as an alphabetical list of the names of the writers, when given. Specifically, they are entered under both subject and name of the writer. Pseudonyms ("Paterfamilias", "Disgusted", etc.) do not count, unless one of them happens to be the *nom de plume* of a columnist (e.g. "Peterborough" of the *Daily Telegraph*), or is otherwise well known:

Apollo 15, achievements of, 125 ltr
Armstrong, Neil, on Apollo 15, 125 ltr

The specific entries for both Leading articles and Letters to the Editor should be distinguished from other index entries. This can best be done by inserting the contracted or abbreviated form (ldr or edl, ltr or corres. for correspondence) either parenthesized at the end of the heading or subheading or else after the reference. Examples of both methods are given above, but whichever method is chosen must be adhered to consistently throughout the index to any one periodical and the meaning of the contraction should be briefly explained ("ldr = Leading article") in the preliminary note.

Reviews of books should be indexed under the generic heading "Book Reviews" if a classified entry is employed. Each subheading consists of the book's full title (excluding any sub-title), followed by the name of the author. The titles can be either in alphabetical order or arranged chronologically according to date of publication. A separate heading can be employed for the subject of the book. At least two other entries are required – the author's name and that of the reviewer. The latter need not recapitulate the titles of the books he has reviewed. Nor need a book title itself have a specific entry unless its publication has attained some exceptional prominence or notoriety that entitles it to its own niche in encyclopaedias. Such a one was *Gone With the Wind* (1936):

BOOK REVIEWS
    Gone With the Wind (Mitchell), revd, 159–60 [NB abbreviation for "reviewed"]
    Mitchell, Margaret, *Gone With the Wind*, revd, 159–60
    Philpots, Jasper, books reviewed by, 97, 159–60, 201

Alternatively, under BOOK REVIEWS the author's name can come before the book's title.

Whether or not obituary notices are grouped under the classified heading Obituaries, it is certain that each of the deceased persons must have his or her own entry:

Philpots, Jasper (literary critic), death of, 358

Many periodicals have other regular features (e.g. bridge, chess, etc.), but their indexing ought to present few special problems.

The indexing of periodical articles

This is really the crux of the matter and upon its excellence or otherwise will depend the entire usefulness of the index. Many (possibly the majority) of periodical indexers confine their entries to the name of the article's author and its title, or words taken from that title. This practice leads almost invariably to a totally inadequate index. For one thing, how many people who have read the article remember its exact title? Again, it makes no allowance for those index users who have not read the article but seek information on some subject matter contained in it. They may say to themselves: "I require information on 'weightlessness in space'", shall we say. "Is there anything about that topic in this periodical?" There *is* a place for an article's title and that is under the author's name. Thus the *Geographic Magazine* in its index for 1965 (if it had had a general index) could have had the following entries for an article entitled "London, all change" (in addition to certain entries for names and subjects):

London: Transport
    Owen, Charles, on, 38 (July), 228–34 ill.[1]
Owen, Charles, "London, all change", 38 (Jul.), 226–34 ill.

But no entry at all, be it noticed, under "London, all change".

[1] It is useful to mark in this way the fact that an article is illustrated, the practice being briefly explained in the index's preliminary note.

Every article in the text, therefore, requires at the very least an index heading for the author (followed by its title) and a subject heading summarizing its main theme. But often a number of other subject headings may also be needed for topics elaborated in the course of the article; these should accordingly be provided, unless a ruthless publisher or editor denies the necessary space. I know, however, of at least two periodicals that are indexed (or were until very recently) quite as fully as any books in their respective fields; they are the photographic magazine *Perspective* and *Ars Quatuor Coronatorum* (or *AQC* for short), a journal of Masonic research.

The quality of the wording of both headings and subheadings is of the utmost importance, especially in the index to a periodical dealing with current affairs, and they must faithfully reflect the tone of the text. The choice of keywords is vital. The main difference in this respect between the indexing of a periodical and that of a monograph is that the headings for the former have to be applicable to the use of different but similar words, or of similar but not identical meanings attached to the same words, by different authors in different contexts. This accentuates the difficulty of "vocabulary control" by the indexer and the need for warning-off signs (or cross-references) from non-adopted terms to the adopted ones. The indexer must either build up his headings and sub-headings progressively, with due circumspection, as and when the need for them arises, or else choose them from a thesaurus. (For thesauri, see pp. 91–2.)

Again, in the course of a periodical's career, words and expressions that have been customarily used as headings may change their meanings or be replaced by other more modern ones. For instance, wireless has become radio, and infantile paralysis is now poliomyelitis, or polio. In any such case it will be necessary, as soon as the new term is introduced in the periodical's text, not only to use that term for the heading in the index entry, but also, for the first year or two following, to provide a "see" cross-reference from the old one.

This applies in particular to cumulated indexes (see Chapter 10), except that now, when the change of terms occurs in the middle of, say, a ten-year cumulation, both the old and the new terms may require their own full entries for the appropriate period, each having a "see also" cross-reference to the other. Otherwise the rule for synonymous subject headings, that one should be chosen for the entry and any others treated merely as cross-references, holds good for periodical indexes as it does in book indexing. Again, specific entry is nearly always preferable to grouping under some system of classification, which is almost invariably inimical to ease and readiness of reference.

Summary

1) The headings in an index to a periodical should as far as possible be "specific entry" rather than classified.

2) Dr J. Edwin Holmstrom, in an important article[1] on this subject, recommends that subject entries should not be confined to what is implicit in the titles of articles; "indexes can be made more effective as aids to stimulating the spread and applications of knowledge if they also pinpoint references that may be of value although occurring only incidentally to the main theme of any given text". To what extent this is practicable will depend on the space available.

3) If not all the names occurring in the text are to be indexed, then the indexer must determine which ones are the more likely to be of value to the user both now and in the future.

4) A similar principle of selectivity may be necessary in the case of subject headings in order to avoid making the index over-full on the one hand and on the other omitting what some types of user may deem essential keywords.

5) The user must not be prevented from finding an item that he is seeking simply because the indexer (probably following the wording of the text) has chosen to use some synonymous term as his keyword. In such cases cross-references will be required:

Ministry, *see* Clergy
Priesthood, *see* Clergy

6) It is equally important to stick consistently to the same keyword even though the writers of various articles employ

[1] "The Indexing of Multi-Author, Multi-Volume and Periodical Publications", *The Indexer*, Vol. 8, No. 1 (April 1972), pp. 31–43.

different terms. In this way will be avoided the serious fault of "scattered information" as exemplified in:

Clergy, 118–23, 135
Ministry, the, 14, 19, 24
Priesthood, the, 236, 243

7) To fulfil most of the above conditions, the indexer must usually have some knowledge of the subject matter of the text.

CHAPTER NINE
Newspaper Indexing

[The index to a newspaper] may, can and must be a good one. There is no longer any excuse for a poor one. Indexing is now an art, not an accident.

James I. Wyer, *Reference Work* (1930)

About 70 million copies of newspaper dailies are distributed in Britain every week. Nearly every paper finds it necessary to maintain an index of its contents, since it is essential for the editor and his staff to be able to trace quickly what has already been said there about any person or topic they may be called upon to discuss in writing. Several years ago John Shaftesley, then Editor of the *Jewish Chronicle* and later Chairman of the Society of Indexers, took six months in preparing a detailed study, by permission of the respective editors and librarians, of the indexes of most of the English national dailies and quality Sunday newspapers, and he included Reuters and the Press Association. He found that their methods varied considerably.

The vast majority of those indexes are compiled solely for internal use. However, some public libraries maintain an index to their local newspaper in order the better to be able to answer queries regarding local affairs (see below).

Owing to the peculiar conditions of a newspaper's production, there are several requirements for its indexing distinct from that of other media.

Procedure

A newspaper index should be kept permanently on cards. According to Harry A. Friedman, who has had considerable experience in this particular branch of indexing, the old loose-leaf and folio index methods are quite obsolete.[1]

The cards vary in size from 2 × 5 in. to 5 × 8 in., but any semi-enamel paper running between 100 and 120 lb to the ream should serve. In order to resist fire, they should be housed in all-steel container cabinets.

There are four methods of indexing newspapers:

1) Direct onto cards from the complete newspaper. The latest edition is usually taken first and all articles and stories to be indexed are marked on it. Then earlier editions are checked so as to include any stories or articles not carried through to the final edition. Unless the indexer is going to do the whole of the work himself, each story and article must be marked with the date, page, column, section and edition – the "reference line".

The papers are then given to typists, who proceed to make fresh cards where none exist to match the marked headings. If such cards already exist, then the new parts of the entries are added to them.

It is also possible for the indexer to type his entries direct on to cards with the newspaper supported on a stand behind the typewriter. This method is illustrated in *News Information* by Geoffrey Whatmore (1964).

2) On cards from cuttings that have already been marked each with the appropriate heading and other matters as above. The file is then consulted and the rest of the procedure is as in (1).

3) On slips, transcribed onto cards – perhaps a week later. This method is reckoned the best for public libraries and for cumulated indexes.

4) On cards with the entries taken from folio notes. But, as the latter will not be in alphabetical order, this precludes rapid transposition of entries.

As Geoffrey Whatmore (op. cit.) points out, many newspaper libraries employ a combination of index and cuttings with the emphasis placed usually on the cuttings. If the indexed newspapers can be retained on microfilm, this arrangement means a great saving of space. If an inquirer merely seeks a date or a name, this can be supplied without recourse to the files.

---

[1] *Newspaper Indexing* (Marquette University Press, Milwaukee, Wisconsin, 1942). Much use is made in this section of the information therein.

Whichever system is used for compiling the index cards, each entry must contain a heading, a subheading or modification in the form of a brief summary of the story or item, and (of course) a reference line:

American Society of Indexers
   affiliated to the British Society
   Feb 24 SUP 7 3

Greek cabinet
   3 members resign
   Jul 13 B 4 5

(For an explanation of the letters and figures, see "The reference line", below.)

The heading

The keyword should almost invariably be taken from one of the words used in the newspaper item being indexed. It must be a word familiar to users. But classification should be avoided. Thus, a reader who seeks information about the Beatles would be unlikely to look under M, as in the following example (taken from an actual index):

Music
  Pop groups
    Beatles
      etc.

Specific entry is almost always preferable to classified headings except perhaps in such matters as Book Reviews, and even here it is desirable to have additional entries for the name of each author, followed by the title of the book.

For verbs in the active voice the present tense is usual:

Prison warders smuggle brandy

For the passive voice a past participle is necessary:

Atkins, Vigor
   nominated Conservative candidate

Every proper name should, to start with, be given an entry,

though some can be discarded later if they prove to be the sole mention of complete nonentities.

Whenever a story deals with a named human being, as do most stories, it is his or her name that should form the principal entry, and when an entry is required for the subject of the story this can often be done by way of cross-reference to the name heading. Only when the subject matter forms the supremely important part of the story can the name headings incidentally connected with it be turned into cross-references.

From the time the index is first prepared, every proper name should have some sort of identification in order to isolate it from similar names that may occur in future issues. Such identification may take one of the following forms:

> title (e.g. Lt-Gen., Rev., Sir)
> occupation (e.g. baker, barrister-at-law, candlestick-maker, magistrates' clerk)
> city or town or country where resident
> place of employment
> street name

Elective office (e.g. MP or Councillor) makes a bad identification as it may soon be lost. Similarly, ranks in the army, navy or air force should be avoided if their holders are still serving, as ranks frequently change on promotion. It is better to use such general titles as army officer, soldier, sailor, seaman, and, if necessary, to resort to additional means of identification:

> Brown, Peter (mechanic, Holbert Lane)
> Brown, Peter (mechanic, Lissom Avenue)

Business firms and companies, if sited in the newspaper's home town, should be identified by the nature of the business:

> Holyoak and Wells (grocer)
> open premises in Lambeth

If not, then by their location:

> Matthews Harness Co. (Brighton)
> reports increased sales

Subject headings and names other than those of persons can often be similarly identified geographically:

Election irregularities (Leeds)
  inquiry reveals marked ballots
Royal Pavilion (Brighton)
  reopened after repairs

Ships' names are not only indexed in italics but are also identified by the parenthesized addition of the type of vessel:

Britannia (ferry)
Britannia (Royal yacht)
Rosemary (tug)
Valiant, HMS (frigate)

Where grouped together in the text, the following can be given classified headings: book reviews, editorials and sports. But a double entry will be required if one of them appears specifically in the text as a news item. In any case, as we have seen, book reviews should be repeated as specific entries under author's name followed by the title of the book.

It may be that in different issues the same subject will be given varied names, e.g.:

Historical Society of Durham
Durham Historical Society
City Historical Society of Durham

and in such a case the original slips will bear each of those names. It is now up to the indexer to ascertain which is the correct one, adopting that for his main entry and furnishing cross-references from the others. A similar treatment is necessary where the same word has varied spellings in different issues (or in the same issue). Consistency in this and other matters is particularly important in newspaper indexing, since each index is likely to be compiled by more than one person – whether simultaneously or in succession to one another – and their terminology should be uniform at any one time, and should remain so for as long as possible.

The first card for any indexable name or subject must contain the heading in full. On subsequent cards it should be ringed round, to prevent its being repeated should the index be reproduced.

Compound phrases that have come to have a universally accepted meaning are never inverted:

Capital punishment	Juvenile delinquency
Colour blindness	Plaster of Paris
Diplomatic immunity	Portland cement
Free trade	Rhodes scholars

It may be, however, that it is sought to invert for the sake of bringing two or more items closely together. Thus, *The Times Index* has:

Living, cost of
Living, standard of

In that case, the headings should be cross-referenced to Cost of living and Standard of living respectively.

Similarly, we can have:

Insurance (*see also* All-risks I., Fire I., Life I., Marine I.)

Descriptive words or phrases used as nicknames are entered only as cross-references:

"Babe" Ruth, *see* Ruth, George Herman ("Babe")

The general practice is to use subject headings for all stories and articles with certain exceptions, which each newspaper office must clearly define. The subject headings should, as far as possible, consist of standardized terms. Technical terms can be entered, but there should be also the ordinary or idiomatic expressions, which will be familiar to the user and should be made the principal entries:

Osteomyelitis, *see* Bone infections

Wherever there is a possible choice, subject headings should be used in the plural form of the word: Murders, Hotels, Fires, Forests, Colorado beetles.

If both the real name of some well-known character and his

pseudonym are equally familiar to the user, enter under real name with cross-reference from pseudonym. If not, then enter under pseudonym:

Olchenitz, M., *see* Verne, Jules (pseud.)

If the pseudonym is less familiar, enter under the real name:

Bell, Currer, *see* Brontë, Charlotte

It is essential that every illustration is incorporated as a heading in the general index since nowadays a whole story may hang upon a single photo-caption, and that story, were it not illustrated, would certainly receive an entry:

Plumpton mine disaster
    survivors helped to surface

Subheadings (or modifications)

Newspaper indexing possesses much in common with headline writing. Both try to isolate, as succinctly as possible, the essentials of the story. Every index heading must have its modification in which that story is told as briefly as possible. Enough of the story should be summarized on the card to avoid the user's having to refer in most cases to the actual newspaper files, or at the least to make it clear that he has struck the right entry.

Every modification should carry a verb, except when it is of a purely routine character, as for instance:

Scottish Crown Courts
    June calendar

It is always best when, together with the heading, each sub-heading can form a complete sentence:

Perlmutter, Pamela				
graduates from Birmingham University	Jul 14	B	2	6
wins title of Miss Coventry	Sep 9		3	4
elopes with College classmate	Dec 17		1	3

(For an explanation of the references, see "The reference line" below.)

It is inadvisable to employ the word "now" in a modification. Thus,

Not	*but*
St Martin's Church	St Martin's Church
now uses revised prayer book	changes to revised prayer book

Advance notices of meetings should not be indexed. Nor is there any need to make an entry for a recorded meeting (unless some importance is attached to the number of meetings held) unless there is some story attached, as for instance:

Willesden Chamber of Commerce
   revises constitution at special meeting

"Conservatives" and "Liberals" are best indexed under the name of their party – Conservative Party (or Conservative & Unionist Party), with cross-references from Unionist Party and Tory Party; and Liberal Party.

Collective nouns can be given a singular verb:

Labour Party
   wins control of borough council

Engagements and marriages are indexed as follows:

Green, Mary
   engaged to Harry White
White, Harry
   engaged to Mary Green

Upon their marriage, the bride and bridegroom's names only appear in the index to mark the actual wedding story, and the entry for the bride's maiden name should take the following form:

Green, Mary (Mrs Harry White)
   see White, Harry

The married name of a famous film star or other careerist should be cross-referred to her better-known name:

Wilcox, Dame Marjorie, *see* Neagle, Anna

A graph in the newspaper text, like any other illustration, must be given an index entry, its style depending upon whether or not the graph itself reveals the whole story. If it does, then such an entry as the following will suffice:

Army recruitment
graph shows trend, 1975–7

But if a further story is disclosed by the graph or its caption, then that must be the chief subject of the subheading:

Army recruitment
increase is due to unemployment (graph)

One final word about subheadings in a newspaper index. They should be arranged line-by-line and not run-on and their order should be chronological, not alphabetical. As regards the second stipulation, however, it will probably prove more convenient to keep together all the allusions to the same story either on the same card or on succeeding cards, even if quite distinct stories relating to the heading appear in the meantime.

The reference line

The third part of the entry is vital. Upon its complete accuracy depends the utility or otherwise of the index. So important is it that it must be allotted the same constant position on each card. Several examples have already been given. Here are two more:

Bank deposits
| 4% gain shown in 1972 | Jan | 5 | 3 | | 2 | 1 | tb |
Motor-car accidents
| prevention campaign starts | Aug | 17 | SUP | | 1 | 5 | pix |

And now for the explanation of the various components. First must come the date, that is the actual printed date of publication (although in the case of provincial weekly newspapers it is often the custom for the papers to appear on the bookstalls a day or two earlier).

For the sake of brevity the following abbreviations are suggested for the names of the months: Jan, Feb, Mar, Apr, May, Jun, Jul, Aug, Sep, Oct, Nov, Dec – or if even greater brevity is desired, then the following are permissible: Ja, F, Mr, Ap, My, Je, Jl, Ag, S, O, N, D. (Note the absence of the final full point, which should normally follow every abbreviation, as opposed to a contraction.) The year is usually stated at the top right-hand corner of each card and serves for all entries in that period. If the index is for two years or part of two years, say 1976–7, then the second year can be placed immediately above the earliest modification connected with it.

Next comes the marking of the number of the edition, usually done by means of symbols in capital letters, B for second edition, C for third and so on. The bulk of the indexing is compiled from a single edition, other editions being used merely to supplement the information or pick up additional stories. If there is no capital letter, the reference can be assumed to be to the first edition. SPE, SUP and FI should be employed to denote Special Edition, Supplement and Final Edition respectively. A starred edition can be denoted by an asterisk.

Then comes the page number, followed by the column number. Where "tb" or "pix" occurs after the column number, those refer to "table" and "illustration" respectively. If either extends to more than one column in the text, this can be shown, e.g. 3–6 pix.

Public libraries and newspaper indexes

In order to be able to answer inquiries, many a public library finds it convenient to maintain an index (or indexes) of the contents of its local newspaper. This will probably consist of *one* general index, as described above; it must be remembered that the fewer indexes, the better – the employment of ten indexes may necessitate the librarian's or other searcher's having to hunt through ten separate sequences.

At the same time, as Geoffrey Whatmore (op. cit.) points out, it may be useful to keep also one or two smaller supplementary records of information constantly in demand. These may include such lists as:

1) Standard Information Index, dealing with subjects like the opening time for admission to notable places; aspects of well-known buildings and geographical features; population statistics and other topics regarding which questions are constantly asked. For instance, tribunals and commissions of inquiry are commonly known by the names of their chairmen, but these are not always

easy to remember, so it is suggested that they be indexed in the following manner:

Civil Service, Report upon, *see* Priestley Report

2) Index of Societies. Names and addresses of secretaries and officials of societies are constantly requested. In the same sequence can be included an Index of Experts (arranged under subject headings). They are worth cultivating because their expertise often provides, direct over the telephone, more useful information, e.g. on technical or medical matters, than can readily be found in printed sources.

3) Index of Sources. Whatmore supplies the following example of subject headings that might be looked for in this index:

Newspapers
    Per head of population, *see Unesco Communications Handbook*

Neither in (1) nor in (3) is there any need to repeat subject headings that are readily available in such sources as *Whitaker's Almanack*.

The Times Index

Although nearly every newspaper in Britain finds it necessary to keep an index in order to be able to refer to its back files, only *The Times*, so far as I am aware, prints and publishes its indexes. It would certainly be a useful venture, although perhaps not a particularly profitable one, if more of the national "quality" daily and Sunday papers were to follow this example. Such indexes would, I believe, be welcomed by the public libraries.

To *The Times Index*, however, must be added *Keesing's Contemporary Archives*, a digest published weekly and indexed at intervals of 2–3 weeks, with regular cumulations. This is particularly useful for picking up foreign and international news. Also the Library Association's *British Humanities Index*, although mainly concerned with periodicals, does include some of the feature articles in *The Times* and the *Guardian*.

The first index to *The Times*, from 1790, was published privately, in instalments, by Samuel Palmer. In 1906 the paper began to publish its own index, which has appeared regularly ever since.

A talk by Mr C. H. J. Kyte, the then Editor of the *Index to The*

Times, given to the Society of Indexers in 1966,[1] contains much interesting information on the production of the index at that time. Since then there have been a number of changes.

The work is currently (early 1978) done by thirteen indexers and an editor. Each indexer uses a printed form which has boxes for date, page, column, prime heading, up to five subheadings, cross-references and abstract. The information on the forms is then typed to produce a punched tape and a print-out, the latter being sent to the indexer for any corrections. The tape is transferred to magnetic tape; this is fed into a computer which sorts the entries into alphabetical order and produces a print-out. This is checked again for possible corrections, before a photosetter films it in page form; from this film a machine plate is cast for printing.

Since 1973 the index has included not only *The Times* but its Educational, Higher Education and Literary supplements, and *The Sunday Times*, including the Colour Magazine.

American newspaper indexes

The principal newspaper index in the USA is that of the *New York Times*, which is now available from 1851 to the present day. (The index has been published regularly since 1913, while earlier indexes intended for editorial use have recently been edited and published.) The index is published twice a month, with an annual cumulation, and is available on subscription.

The entries are usually made under the most specific headings, but there are some deliberate exceptions to this, and careful study of the preliminary note is essential.

Unlike newspaper indexes for editorial use, the index goes into considerable detail. As the preliminary note observes: "Entries are by no means limited to a minimal indication of the general content of the item from which they derive . . ." One example, from the index of 1975, may suffice. Under "Travel – United States" the following subheading appears:

> Computerized information index, called Trav-L-Dex, capable of storing details on 500,000 tours, travel packages, cruises and hotels, is scheduled to go into operation Feb 1 in New Eng, NY, NJ, Ill, Calif, Tex and Washington state (S), D 21, X, p5.

[1] *The Indexer*, Vol. 5, No. 3 (Spring 1967), pp. 125–9.

The reference at the end means, of course, December 21st, while the X, and other roman numerals in the index, indicate various Sunday supplements other than the main news section of the paper. The bracketed S is a "story length indicator", meaning "a short item of half a column or less", the other length indicators used being M and L. There are cross-references to this subheading under "Indexes and Indexing" and "Trav-L-Dex".

Another notable indexing project is the Newspaper Index published by the Newspaper Indexing Center, part of the Micro Photo Division of the Bell & Howell Company of Wooster, Ohio. Formerly a single index covering four important newspapers, this now comprises separate indexes to several papers, each index being published monthly with an annual cumulation. The papers indexed include the *Chicago Tribune*, the *Houston Post*, the *Los Angeles Times*, the *New Orleans Times-Picayune*, the *San Francisco Chronicle*, and the *Washington Post*.

Each of the Bell & Howell indexes is in two parts, a subject index and a personal name index. In general, the entries are specific, but, as the preliminary note explains: "Corporations, organizations and various social institutions (hospitals, libraries, schools . . .) are filed under the generic subject. . . . If the volume of entries . . . becomes too large [the subject] may be removed from the generic subject heading and refiled under its own name." In such cases, cross-references are given.

National, international, regional, state and local news are all indexed, as are letters to the editors and certain other features, but the indexes are primarily intended to cover news reported in the USA, and foreign news is usually indexed under country of origin rather than by subject.

CHAPTER TEN

Cumulative Indexing

To add golden numbers to golden numbers.
Thomas Dekker (1570–1641),
Patient Grissell

If cumulative indexing consisted merely of supplying additional page-reference numbers (however golden), there would have been no need for this chapter. But the task is rather more complex.

A cumulative index has been defined[1] as follows: "Where a book is published in several volumes, each with its own index, or where a periodical is provided with an index each year or part of a year, and these separate indexes are combined to form an index to a/the whole series, the product is called a cumulative index."

In one sense, of course, owing to the nature of the work, every index is a cumulative effort. But that is not what the term signifies. The compilation of a cumulative index implies that there are several indexes in existence already and that those, perhaps with the addition of one for the final volume, must be merged to form one composite index.

The need applies equally to multi-volumed books, to periodicals and to newspapers, although a cumulation of more than one year's index for a daily newspaper is seldom practicable. Nothing can be more time-wasting than to have to search through, say, twenty years' issues of a periodical of which there are two volumes a year.

For many years the Reference, Special and Information Section of the Library Association campaigned to persuade publishers of scientific and technical journals to issue cumulative indexes; with limited success, however, mainly because of the cost. Among the

---

[1] *Training in Indexing*, p. 9.

few British periodicals that already perform this useful service must be mentioned *The Engineer*; *Notes & Queries*; and *International Associations*. In the United States the H. W. Wilson Company publishes several periodical indexes.

All newspapers and most periodicals that are already indexed would undoubtedly be rendered more serviceable for the researcher if their indexes were cumulated – newspapers, say, once a year and periodicals every five or ten years. The problem here is mainly economic; how many people would be prepared to buy the finished product? The cumulation would, therefore, have to be made for internal use. With technical journals there is a further problem. Here, says Mr L. E. J. Helyar,[1]

> there is a decreasing value in much of the contents as it loses its currency. A certain amount of the material is detail which has day-to-day significance . . . but loses all but historical significance under the impact of new technical advances. This means a cumulative index covering more than a very few years would probably not be economically justified.

What books need cumulative indexes? I should say that any indexed multi-volume work, or at any rate any that comprises more than three volumes, ought to have one, either as part of the final volume or (if necessary) in a separate volume of its own. This applies particularly to histories, biographies and belles-lettres.

The technique

The index to the first volume to be cumulated is important because it will set the standard for the rest of the work. But the cumulator must not feel deterred from making changes where he considers that the original indexer's methods have been misconceived, or again in his own system as he progresses. For instance, in compiling a cumulated medical index he may have made a main entry under Mongolism and relegated its synonym, Down's syndrome, to a cross-reference; but then, shall we say in Vol. 6, he comes across a whole article or chapter entitled "Down's syndrome" and this will necessitate his reversing his procedure:

Down's syndrome (Mongolism)
   [subheadings]
Mongolism, *see* Down's syndrome

[1] *The Indexer,* Vol. 2, No. 4 (Autumn 1961), p. 137.

It must be remembered that there is seldom, if ever, time to read through the whole text, as is recommended in the case of an ordinary index; although, of course, if the cumulator is the same person as the original indexer, he will at least be familiar with the text of the various volumes. But it still remains necessary to check each individual index entry with the text before including it in the cumulation. In this way not only can the accuracy of the references be ensured but it may also be possible to eliminate superfluous entries or sub-entries. Thus, if it were found, for example, that the following statement:

> Research undertaken on psychosis in adolescents and in adults, but not in children, showed that . . .

had been indexed as a "Psychosis" subheading to an entry under "Children", or as a "Children" subheading under "Psychosis" or "Research", or (worse still) under all three, then those entirely negative sub-entries could be thrown out at once, unless, of course, the fact that no research was undertaken on children was relevant to the findings. Such is the experience of Mrs M. L. Osborn, whose cumulative indexes to the *Modern perspectives in psychiatry* series have been highly praised.[1]

It may be easy to cut out each entry in the successive indexes and paste them in alphabetical order on to large sheets of paper (A4, perhaps), being careful to leave a sufficient space between each entry for the possible insertion of subheadings where otherwise the reference numbers would exceed, say, five. The subsequent repetitions of the original heading will of course have to be ringed round. Some entries will naturally occur only once each.

If copies of the indexes themselves (offprints, it may be) are not available, photostats may be used instead. Alternatively, the index may be written out by hand or typed onto cards; or it may be typed onto sheets of paper which are then cut up, the resulting slips being alphabetized. There is something to be said for working with cards or large slips of paper rather than the tiny slips that result from cutting up the original indexes.

The choice of word or words to serve as a heading is of considerable importance, although, as explained above, this may have

---

[1] *The Indexer,* Vol. 8, No. 3 (April 1973), p. 180.

to be changed in the course of cumulation. But when this is so and the discarded entry heading was chosen out of some expression in the text, a reader may reasonably expect to find it referred to in the index. Consequently it must be retained as a cross-reference.

A greater difficulty arises when organizations or countries change their names during the process of cumulation. For instance, during the process of cumulation of one two-year volume of *Keesing's Contemporary Archives*,

> four states of the former French West Africa (Senegal, French Sudan, Dahomey and Upper Volta)) decided to form the Mali Federation; while later two (Dahomey and Upper Volta) withdrew; then with great pomp and ceremony the remaining two members (Senegal and French Sudan) proclaimed officially their fusion and independence as the Mali Federation; within two months Senegal seceded from the Federation, which then ceased to exist, its remaining member (French Sudan) adopting the designation "The Republic of Mali".[1]

Recurrent entries

Recurrent material must be traced through all the numbers of the periodical, or through all the volumes of the book, for which the cumulated index is being prepared, and comprehensive entries prepared. In doing so, consistency in form and punctuation is essential. For instance, in the text of a symposium the name of a certain Dr Jasper Marmaduke Philpots may occur at different places in varying forms. One might have:

> Philpots, J. M.; Philpots, Jasper M.; Philpots, Jasper; Philpots, J.; Philpots, Dr; Philpots, Dr Jasper; Philpots, Dr Jasper M.; Philpots, Dr J. M.; Philpots, Dr J.

In any such case, the variants must be sorted out – this may call for some research in the text by way of identifying the references – and the most suitable form decided upon. In the above collection this would be Philpots, J. M., unless he happens to be one of those people who are almost invariably referred to by one of their forenames in conjunction with the surname, when it would be Philpots, Jasper M., or if it were the second forename, then I would suggest Philpots, (J.) Marmaduke.

---

[1] *The Indexer*, Vol. 2, No. 3 (Spring 1961), pp. 81–2.

References and cross-references

As Robert J. Palmer, a well-known New York indexer, has pointed out (in a private communication), it is essential that a reference appears at only one place in any cumulative index. In other words, there should be extensive use of "see" and "see also" cross-references so that there is only one logical place in the index for any one piece of information. If this is not done, the references in different parts of the index that should normally be mirror images of each other gradually differ more and more. In an ordinary index this can be controlled on the cards or in the typing, but a cumulative index will gradually get out of control unless a rigorous principle of non-duplication of references is followed throughout.

The references in a cumulated index to a periodical need careful attention. As I mentioned in Chapter 8, each issue (or each annual volume) may begin again at page 1, so that the indexer will need to indicate the volume number or year, perhaps both, in addition to the page reference. It may also be necessary to indicate the month, or the number of the issue, depending on the system of pagination that has been followed.

Terminology

A further problem is connected with the terminology of headings. The same text may contain, sometimes at widely separated intervals, allusions to river-beds, river beds and even riverbeds. One form, say River-beds, must be firmly selected and adopted for the index entry. Relating her experiences in compiling a cumulated index to the first eight volumes of that learned periodical, *The Cartographic Journal*, Brenda Hall[1] selects the expression "automation" (in cartography):

> Scarcely touched on in Volume 1, it is getting under way in Volumes 2 and 3, and is in full flood by Volume 4. It starts to splinter into separate concepts. Automation applied to cartography becomes automated cartography, computer mapping, automated plotting, automated draughting, automated contouring, and so forth. Even the most intuitive indexer cannot always foresee how subjects will develop. Solutions to this problem are at the root and heart of successful cumulative indexing.

[1] "A Computer-generated Index Technique", *The Indexer*, Vol. 8, No. 3 (April 1973), pp. 130–8.

Had it been my decision to make, I should have been inclined to provide a heading for Automated cartography, *see also under* Plotting; Draughting; Contouring. For Computer mapping I should give a "see" cross-reference to Automated cartography. (That is, relying entirely on Miss Hall's statement and without my knowing the number of references involved.)

It is possibly the above splintering capacity of subject headings that prompted Wheatley, in the concluding paragraph of his pioneering work *How to Make an Index* which forms his sole allusion to cumulative indexing, to give the piece of advice:

> In making a general index of several volumes, always index the volumes afresh, and do not be contented with using what has been done before. It is always better to put "new wine into new bottles".

Periodical cumulations for editorial use

As has already been pointed out, only in a very few cases can the cost of printing a cumulated index be afforded for a periodical. But quite often will an editor require for his own use a manuscript or typed cumulation. This may involve the issues of up to twenty years (that is, as many as 240 in the case of a monthly) and consequently is no light task. As G. H. Burns has shown,[1] what is needed in most cases is a single card index complete in itself up to the date of compilation and lending itself readily to the making of additions continuously or at suitable intervals. As a result of the end product's not being intended for publication, there is virtually no restriction on the amount of space available, while it is usually possible for the indexer to quote any reasonable period for completion with "every prospect of obtaining agreement". Again, there are no printers' "deadlines" to work to, although naturally a freelance indexer (if one is employed) should perform his task with reasonable promptitude.

In making this species of cumulated index it must be remembered that the motto "think of the user", which has been stressed throughout this volume, applies in the present instance not to the general readership of the journal so much as to the editorial staff. Personalities are quite likely to assume significance at a later date

---

[1] "Journal Indexes – for Editorial Use", *The Indexer*, Vol. 8, No. 1 (April 1972), pp. 62–5.

when the editor wishes to record them in connexion with some event. Mr Burns recommends that a name entry should be provided and also one under the particular interest associated with that person, in order to facilitate future retrieval. As planning ahead figures largely in every editor's day, no subject entry that can have any bearing on this part of his work should on any account be omitted. For the same reason a chronological arrangement of sub-headings, rather than an alphabetical one, is almost always to be preferred.

A general heading can sometimes be usefully employed for some term which is not itself to be found in the text. For instance, a journal may have a hobbies section, which over a period could include papers on Oil Painting, Sculpture, Woodcarving, Lapidary, etc. Those could be gathered together under a classified "Arts and crafts" heading, the subheadings being confined to cross-references to those specific main entries.

In the case of cumulative indexes for general office use it is advisable that the entries should be typed onto cards that are punched with a hole near the base, and the whole set maintained in similarly holed drawers through which lockable metal rods protrude. Otherwise it will be found that the index (or parts of it) is apt to disappear into the staff's private files.

CHAPTER ELEVEN
Editing the Index

When the indexer comes to the last page of a great book he rejoices to have finished his work; but he will find by experience, when he calculates the arrangement of his materials, that he has scarcely done more than half of what is before him.

Wheatley, *How to Make an Index*

Wheatley's warning is necessary for anyone who imagines that once he has made his last index entry all he has to do is to sit back, relax, and wait for the cheque to come through his letter-box. Two tasks remain to be done, although my experience suggests that usually together they do not consume as much as one half of the time taken so far on the whole job.

First, the index manuscript must be edited and prepared as suitable "copy" for the printer. Then, some weeks, perhaps, after he has sent off the fruits of his labours to the publisher, the indexer may receive the printed proofs of the index to be read through for any necessary corrections. Proof-correction will be dealt with in the next chapter.

As regards the form in which the index should be sent to the publisher for transmission to the printer, it can either be type-written on sheets of paper (usually quarto or A4) or else sent on the index cards (or slips, including gummed slips) on which it was compiled.

If the index is typed – and this will be essential if it has been compiled in an alphabetized notebook – the following rules should be observed:

1) Double spacing, with typing on one side of the paper only.
2) Ample margins, especially on the left-hand side.

3) Pages to be numbered consecutively, preferably in the top right-hand corner.
4) Top copy to be sent and carbon copy retained.

Printers prefer to work from typed pages, and often refer to cards or slips as "rough copy", for using which they charge extra. The reason is obvious. On the composing machine a reading rack is arranged on which the compositor rests his copy. If every time he comes to the end of one card (probably, more often than not, containing only one or two lines) he has to take it off and replace it with another from the pile on the table, the job is going to take considerably longer.

However, instances of a printer's refusing to accept a neat and legible set of index cards seem to be rare. Should this happen, the cards can be pasted on to paper, often as many as ten to a page.

Perhaps I ought to mention that personally I always use cards in preference to slips. They are more expensive, but they can mostly be used three or four times. I also like to have my index always standing in order between alphabetical markers in a special box, so that I can look at once to see whether a subject has occurred before in the book's text, and, if necessary, add a subheading or a fresh page reference. I always type the original heading on the card as well as all subheadings, adding extra page numbers in ink. In this way the index is constantly complete (apart from the final editing) as far as it has gone. Also much of the editing can be done, so to speak, *en route*.

In editing an index the following "nine points of editing" need to be watched for.

1) Alphabetical arrangement

It is quite a simple matter for a card[1] to have strayed into the wrong order in its own letter of the alphabet, or even into a different letter. If it is left there, the compositor will surely print it where it stands, and corrections will be necessary on the proofs. Since the cost of such corrections, especially in page proof, can run into money, the alphabetical order should be checked very carefully.

---

[1] Subsequent references in this chapter to cards refer also to slips.

2) *Correct spelling throughout*

This speaks for itself. But perhaps I may be allowed a digression which barely concerns editing but does raise a point not much stressed in the foregoing chapters. It is that the indexer is in an ideal position to detect errors and discrepancies in the text of the book he is indexing – discrepancies which may easily have escaped the notice of both author and publisher's editor, such as a name being spelt in more than one way.

On various occasions I have found myself in almost daily telephone communication with the author or the publisher regarding queries or suggested corrections – by no means merely of spelling. This is no part of the indexer's job (unless he has been expressly commissioned to correct the proofs). But experience has shown that it is usually welcomed by the publisher's editor, who is not averse to having an additional, unpaid proof-reader. Also, an indexer who takes pride in his work will wish the text of all books on which he has laboured to be as nearly perfect as possible.

3) *Typography*

There is much that wants watching here. All words that are to be in italics (e.g. titles of books, periodicals, operas and long poems; names of ships; foreign words and "see" and "see also") must be underlined.

Quotation marks ("quotes") are normally used when citing titles of: articles in magazines; chapters of books; essays; paintings and sculptures; songs and shorter poems; and sometimes the names of hotels and inns, when these do not form part of a title. The indexer should, of course, follow the usage of the text.

If the main references are to be differentiated by having their page numbers printed in bold type, the references should be underlined with a wavy line.

Again, if headings are to be printed in capitals and small capitals, they must be appropriately marked.

4) *Punctuation*

Commas must be correctly and consistently placed. There must be a comma between every reference or group of references (by "group" is meant, for example, "141–2"), though some indexers prefer to dispense with the comma before the first reference, substituting an appropriate space after the end of the words of headings or subheadings (see pp. 59–60).

On no account must a comma be used after a main heading which is not immediately followed by page references, but only by subheadings. If a run-on system is used, a colon must be placed after the main heading. This very important rule is sometimes ignored, with resulting ambiguity (see pp. 60–1).

Where the run-on system is adopted for subheadings, each subheading must be separated by a semi-colon. In the line-by-line system subheadings are taken care of by indentation:

Churches
    abbey, 839, 972
    basilican, 538
    Byzantine, 753

Full stops are not to be used in an index except (a) to mark an abbreviation, and perhaps (b) before "see also".

5) *Subheadings*

The following rule does not apply to typewritten indexes, but only to those submitted on cards, where subheadings may extend to several cards. The main heading will have to be repeated on each of them, but should be circled on the second or subsequent cards; otherwise it will almost certainly be printed each time, necessitating expensive correction on the proofs.

6) *Too many page numbers in a row*

Long "strings" of page references should be examined afresh. About seven references should be the absolute limit (except after the subheading "other references"), and fewer are recommended.

Excessive page references can be avoided by the use of subheadings, with a final "other references" for the more trivial items. If a subheading itself has the extra page numbers, then there can be either sub-subheadings or (and preferably, in the case of indexing general literature) just "see . . ." with the topic itself made into a separate heading, with its own subheadings (see p. 106).

7) *Cross-references*

It is important during editing to make sure that each cross-reference does refer to a heading that actually appears in the index and has page numbers following it. Nothing is more infuriating to the index user than to draw a complete blank or to find that a cross-reference merely refers him to another:

Braun, von, *see* Von Braun
Von Braun, *see* Braun, von

To facilitate ease of research, "see" references should be avoided unless there are more than three page numbers or some sub-headings. It is better to repeat the page references under each heading (see p. 111). The important thing in editing such entries is to see that all the page numbers are shown in each entry and that they all correspond.

It is also important to ensure that there is no conflict between entries and "see also" cross-references.

8) *Scattered information*

Other errors to be looked for when editing are instances where information has been split or scattered among synonymous or related headings instead of being grouped under the same heading; or again where similar information has been indexed at different hierarchical levels.

9) *Preliminary note*

The use of special symbols, or abbreviations; the printing of certain page numbers in bold type or italics; the use of *bis* and *ter* after a page reference; or the use of (a) and (b) or (i) and (ii) to indicate different columns in the text – all these need to be explained in a preliminary note at the beginning of the index. Similarly, any other unconventional features should be explained. This certainly forms part of the editing process.

The following note which appeared at the beginning of an index to a biography may be fairly typical.

The name of Winston Churchill occurs on almost every page of the text. To avoid unnecessary overloading, the entry under his name has not been made a table of contents of the entire volume but has been confined to those headings which cannot be readily found under other entries.

Throughout the index his name has been abbreviated to WSC and that of his son, the author, to RSC.

Large and small Capitals for a surname denote that it is the subject of a short biography between page xxv and page xxxvi.

Page numbers in **bold type** indicate that more than a few lines are devoted to the subject in the text. Reference numbers in *italics* indicate illustrations or their captions, or maps. *q.v.* stands for *quod vide* ("which see").

bis after a reference number denotes that the item is quite separately mentioned twice on the same page of the text, and *ter* three times; "q." stands for "quoted"; *passim* denotes that the references are scattered throughout the pages indicated.

Subheadings have been arranged mainly in chronological order. The method of alphabetical order is word-by-word.

The novice indexer may ask: Nine points of editing? Surely all this work is not really necessary before the index is submitted? Can it not be sent as it stands and necessary corrections made on the proofs? The answer is: of course, they could be, but the operation might prove enormously expensive and also delay the publication of the book. The aim of editing should be to have a manuscript so intelligible and so perfectly prepared that the only mistakes to be corrected in the proofs will be those of the printer.

As with so many other things, speed in editing comes with practice, and the experienced indexer can be found flicking through his cards at a fairly fast rate. Except in the case of the very largest indexes, a single day's work should suffice to carry out the whole process comfortably.

Although typographical instructions to the printer are the responsibility of the publisher's production department, there is at least one general instruction that the indexer can usefully give. If it is put at the top of the typescript when the index is submitted, it must be circled to show that it is not to be printed:

When paging the proofs please ensure that, where subheadings extend from one page to the next, the main heading is repeated at the top of the following page, followed by "(continued)".

This practice makes all the difference to an index's usefulness and appearance, but is very often omitted unless the printer is reminded.

Other instructions may sometimes be marked by the indexer, by arrangement with the publisher; for example, when the indexer has indicated the use of bold face or some other special typographical feature.

One final point remains to be checked, when the indexer is satisfied with the work in other respects (though he will have paid some attention to it from the beginning): its length. It is sad but true that the publisher's editor, left with a certain number of pages blank and the rest of the book in proof, may pay as much attention to the length of the index as to its quality. As we saw in Chapter 2, there may be some discrepancy between the ideal length of the index and the space available for it. Even though it may be transparently obvious that the publisher really ought to have allowed more pages in the first place, it remains part of the indexer's job to help solve the problem that has presented itself, which entails tailoring the index to the space available as best he can.

CHAPTER TWELVE

The Correction of Proofs

If life had a second edition, how would I correct the proofs!
John Clare

Essential though it is, reading the proofs is not the most interesting part of index-making. Nevertheless, indexers should, in my opinion, always offer to correct the proofs of their indexes. Many publishers send the proofs without question. Usually two copies are sent, but only one need be returned.

The proofs reach the indexer in one of two forms. They are either long "galley" sheets, unpaged, or else page proofs, which again may be either paged galleys or ordinary pages; sometimes the page proofs are bound up elaborately with the text of the book into a rough paperback.

Whole lines may be safely added or deleted on ordinary galleys, but this should never be attempted on page proofs without full compensation in the same column, or at least on the same page. Otherwise succeeding pages of the index may have to be remade up, at great expense. In the same way, in the case of a long set of run-on subheadings, the insertion or deletion of a whole word should be avoided except in the last line or two, since otherwise resetting of many lines, or of the entire paragraph, may be necessary.

One may ask why such stringent precautions are necessary. They are required because of the enormous expense of making corrections on the printed page. It is impossible to give an exact idea of what the cost of corrections would be at the present time, since, with different methods of setting, the cost of altering a single line can vary from less than 50p to £2.

Consequently, at the page-proof stage trivial verbal amendments are rarely worth while, and when the indexer is tempted he should bear in mind Sir Francis Bacon's dictum: "The most corrected copies are commonly the least correct." The time for making corrections is when editing one's script for the press.

Now for the actual work of proof-reading. There are two classes of corrections: those due to printer's errors and those which are "author's corrections" – either mistakes in the indexer's original copy (but if he carefully edited it, there should be none), or after-thoughts. It is customary to use inks of different colour to distinguish these two classes of corrections, the usual scheme being red for printer's errors and blue for author's corrections.

The proofs will often be found to contain marginal notes from the printer's reader, querying ambiguities, inconsistencies, or possible inaccuracies. If he agrees with a suggestion from the printer, the indexer strikes out the reader's question mark. If not, he strikes out the suggested alteration as well.

Sometimes an unfamiliar touch in the proof will reveal, on examination of the typescript (the indexer having prudently kept a carbon copy), that the publisher's editor has himself taken a hand by "improving" or "tampering with" (according to the point of view) the indexer's work. Such a case calls for the greatest tact, but if the indexer does not consider the amendment to be an improvement, he should at least inquire the reason for it. He may learn that he has infringed one of the house rules of the firm concerned.

Proof-reading should be carried out by scanning the index, line by line, for possible errors. Each line of the proof should be carefully checked against the original typescript, and special care should be taken in checking the page references, since there is a higher rate of typographical errors in numbers than in letters and any mistakes are usually more damaging. Except in case of doubt, it should rarely be necessary to refer to the text of the book. A commonly adopted method of focusing the attention on one line at a time is to place a ruler or sheet of paper on the page, moving it downwards line by line.

Sometimes the text of the book will be altered in proof, while the indexer is working from an uncorrected proof, or even after he has delivered his index, and publishers' editors have been known to overlook the consequent need for correction of the index. This can result in the omission of important subjects that certainly ought to have been included, or, conversely, of the inclusion in the index of items that do not appear in the printed book. If repaging is entailed, the index proofs may contain errors in page references that were perfectly correct when the indexer originally noted them. Incorrect page references in the index sometimes fall into a pattern that can alert the indexer to what must have happened.

Ideally, the indexer should see the final corrected proofs of the book, so that he can amend the index accordingly; but this is not always easy to arrange, unless the indexer can drop everything and present himself at the publisher's office just when the corrected proofs are ready for the printer. It sometimes helps just to inquire about the possibility of seeing corrected proofs of the text, so as to alert the editor to the possibility that he may have to make corrections to the index himself.

When marking corrections on the proofs, the standard symbols for proof-correction should always be used. These are shown in the table below.

NOTES ON THE USE OF SYMBOLS FOR CORRECTING PROOFS

All corrections should be distinct and made in ink in the margins; marks made in the text should be those indicating the place to which the correction refers.

Where several corrections occur in one line, they should be divided between the left and right margins, the order being from left to right in both margins, and the individual marks should be separated by a concluding mark.

When an alteration is desired in a character, word or words, the existing character, word or words should be struck through, and the character to be substituted written in the margin followed by a /.

Where it is desired to change one character only to a capital letter, the word 'cap' should be written in the margin. Where, however, it is desired to change more than one character, or a word or words, in a particular line to capitals, then one marginal reference, 'caps', should suffice, with the appropriate symbols made in the text as required.

Three periods or full stops (constituting an ellipsis, see No. 61) should be used to indicate an omission, except where the preceding sentence has been concluded, in which case *four* full stops should be inserted, the first of which should be close up to the preceding word.

Normally, only matter actually to be inserted or added to the existing text should be written on the proof. If, however, any comments or instructions are written on the proof, they should be encircled, and preceded by the word PRINTER (in capitals and underlined).

(Words printed in italics in the marginal marks column below are instructions and not part of the marks).

SYMBOLS FOR CORRECTING PROOFS

No.	Instruction	Textual mark	Marginal mark
1	Correction is concluded	None	/
2	Insert in text the matter indicated in margin	ʎ	*New matter followed by* /
3	Delete	Strike through characters to be deleted	ℐ
4	Delete and close up	Strike through characters to be deleted and use mark 21	ℐ
5	Leave as printed	. . . . under characters to remain	*stet*
6	Change to italic	——— under characters to be altered	*ital*

No.	Instruction	Textual mark	Marginal mark
7	Change to even small capitals	≡≡≡ under characters to be altered	*s.c.*
8	Change to capital letters	≡≡≡ under characters to be altered	*caps*
9	Use capital letters for initial letters and small capitals for rest of words	≡≡ under initial letters and ≡≡ under the rest of the words	*c. & s.c.*
10	Change to bold type	∿ under characters to be altered	*bold*
11	Change to lower case	Encircle characters to be altered	*l.c*
12	Change to roman type	Encircle characters to be altered	*rom*
13	Wrong fount. Replace by letter of correct fount	Encircle character to be altered	*w.f.*
14	Invert type	Encircle character to be altered	↻
15	Change damaged character(s)	Encircle character(s) to be altered	✗
16	Substitute or insert character(s) under which this mark is placed, in 'superior' position	/ through character or ∧ where required	⌐ *under character (e.g. $\frac{x}{\curlyvee}$)*
17	Substitute or insert character(s) over which this mark is placed, in 'inferior' position	/ through character or ∧ where required	∧ *over character (e.g. $\widehat{x}$)*
18	Underline word or words	——— under words affected	*underline*
19	Use ligature (e.g. ffi) or diphthong (e.g. œ)	⌢⌣ enclosing letters to be altered	⌢⌣ *enclosing ligature or diphthong required*

No.	Instruction	Textual mark	Marginal mark
20	Substitute separate letters for ligature or diphthong	/ through ligature or diphthong to be altered	*write out separate letters followed by* /
21	Close up—delete space between characters	⁔ linking characters	⁔
22	Insert space*	⋏	#
23	Insert space between lines or paragraphs*	> between lines to be spaced	#
24	Reduce space between lines*	(connecting lines to be closed up	*less* #
25	Make space appear equal between words	| between words	*eq* #
26	Reduce space between words*	| between words	*less* #
27	Add space between letters*	⏐⏐⏐⏐⏐ between tops of letters requiring space	*letter* #
28	Transpose	⌐⌐ between characters or words, numbered when necessary	*trs*
29	Place in centre of line	Indicate position with ⌐　　⌐	*centre*
30	Indent one em	⌐	▯
31	Indent two ems	⌐⌐	▭
32	Move matter to right	⌐ at left side of group to be moved	⌐
33	Move matter to left	⌐ at right side of group to be moved	⌐

* Amount of space and/or length of re-spaced line may be indicated.

No.	Instruction	Textual mark	Marginal mark
34	Move matter to position indicated	[ ] at limits of required position	*move*
35	Take over character(s) or line to next line, column or page	⌐	*take over*
36	Take back character(s) or line to previous line, column or page	⌐	*take back*
37	Raise lines*	⌅ over lines to be moved ⌄ under lines to be moved	*raise*
38	Lower lines*	⌐ over lines to be moved ↓ under lines to be moved	*lower*
39	Correct the vertical alignment	‖	‖
40	Straighten lines	══ through lines to be straightened	══
41	Push down space	Encircle space affected	⊥
42	Begin a new paragraph	⌐ before first word of new paragraph	*n.p.*
43	No fresh paragraph here	⌒ between paragraphs	*run on*
44	Spell out the abbreviation or figure in full	Encircle words or figures to be altered	*spell out*
45	Insert omitted portion of copy NOTE. The relevant section of the copy should be returned with the proof, the omitted portion being clearly indicated.	⋏	*out see copy*
46	Substitute or insert comma	/ through character or ⋏ where required	,/
47	Substitute or insert semi-colon	/ through character or ⋏ where required	;/

* Amount of space and/or length of line may be included.

No.	Instruction	Textual mark	Marginal mark
48	Substitute or insert full stop	/ through character or ⋏ where required	⊙
49	Substitute or insert colon	/ through character or ⋏ where required	⊙
50	Substitute or insert interrogation mark	/ through character or ⋏ where required	?/
51	Substitute or insert exclamation mark	/ through character or ⋏ where required	!/
52	Insert parentheses	⋏ or ⋏ ⋏	(/)/
53	Insert (square) brackets	⋏ or ⋏ ⋏	[/]/
54	Insert hyphen	⋏	|-|
55	Insert en (half-em) rule	⋏	en
56	Insert one-em rule	⋏	em
57	Insert two-em rule	⋏	2 em
58	Insert apostrophe	⋏	⸜
59	Insert single quotation marks	⋏ or ⋏ ⋏	⸜ ⸜
60	Insert double quotation marks	⋏ or ⋏ ⋏	⸜⸜ ⸝⸝
61	Insert ellipsis*	⋏	.../
62	Insert leader	⋏	⊙⋯
63	Insert shilling stroke	⋏	⊘
64	Refer to appropriate authority anything of doubtful accuracy	Encircle words, etc. affected	?

* See notes on use of symbols.

CHAPTER THIRTEEN
Humour in Indexing

One of the last things the genuine indexer thinks
of is to make his work amusing . . .

Wheatley, *How to Make an Index*

The quotation at the head of this chapter is taken from the first
sentence of Wheatley's chapter on "Amusing and Satirical Indexes", for, despite his opening asseveration, Wheatley was able
to find a good deal of wit and satire in the indexes to the *Tatler* and
Spectator, and in the works of Leigh Hunt, John Gay, and others.
An entry such as "London, its happiness before the invention of
Coaches and Chairs"[1] induces a wry smile in our traffic-conscious
age, but the appeal of "Flattery of women, its ill consequences"[2]
seems timeless.

For other examples of humour in early indexes I refer my
readers to Wheatley's excellent books, which are available in good
libraries and may sometimes be obtained at second hand. Here, I
confine myself in the main to examples of deliberate humour in
twentieth-century indexes, though I have appended a few brief
notes on unconscious humour in indexing and on some humorous
comments on indexing.

The clerihew

In 1905 there appeared the original book of clerihews, *Biography
for Beginners*, by E. Clerihew (the pseudonym of E. C. Bentley),
with "diagrams" by G. K. Chesterton. The introductory note to

---

[1] From Gay's *Poems* (1720).   [2] From *The Tatler*.

the index (which, by the way, is headed "Index of Psychology"), reads:

In all work of a biographic character it is important to make copious reference to as many as possible of the generally-recognized virtues, vices, good points, foibles, peculiarities, tricks, characteristics, little weaknesses, traits, imperfections, fads, idiosyncrasies, singularities, morbid symptoms, oddities, faults, and regrettable propensities set forth in the following table. The form of an alphabetic index, with references to the examples given in the preceding pages, has been chosen, so that the beginner who may be desirous, when trying his hand at work of this sort, of seeing how any given one of these subjects may best be treated, is enabled at once to turn to one or more model passages.

Each clerihew has one or more entries in the index, and one has an entry under every letter of the alphabet – that on Sir Christopher Wren:

Sir Christopher Wren
Said, "I am going to dine with some men.
If anybody calls
Say I am designing St. Paul's."

This is indexed under: Abominable deceit; Bankruptcy, moral; Conduct, disingenuous; Domestic servants, encouragement of dishonesty among; Escutcheon, blot on, action involving; Fact, cynical perversion of; etc., etc., ending with: Veracity, departure from; World, the next, neglect of prospects in; Y.M.C.A., unfitness for; and Zealous pursuit of pleasure at expense of soul.

How to be useful and happy

Humour of a different kind is to be found in the index to A. Lapthorn Smith's *How to be useful and happy from sixty to ninety* (John Lane, 1922), in which the author's perfectly serious intention informs every entry. "To overcome the erroneous idea that because a man has reached the age of sixty he must give up all his interests in life and spend the rest of his days in idleness and sorrow is the object of this modest little book", he writes (pp. 4–5), and his index is a fascinating blend of serious indexing, deliberate humour, and some remarkable examples of accidental humour deriving from his very shaky technique. I assume that Lapthorn Smith did in fact intend his readers to be able to find the information they wanted, when looking in the index for a particular subject; but it may be that his index was, rather, intended to be read for its own sake. At all events, he breaks several rules of indexing, being guilty of scattered information, defective double entry, and atrociously bad choice of keywords, in the course of producing an index that is a delight to read or to dip into:

Absurdity of voluntary retirement at sixty, 5
Adding ten years to life, 218
Alcohol as cure for insomnia, very bad, 190
All day in garden at 103, 44 [not indexed under Garden(ing)]
Beard, long white, don't wear, 56
Busy doctor at ninety, 5, 6 [also indexed under Doctor, with reference to p. 6 only]
Carriage and pair shortens life, 68
Cause of insomnia must be found, 188
Cook, good, source of danger to elderly men, 69
Crime to die rich, 112
Engine drivers over sixty, what to do with them, 44
Gardening at one hundred, 106
Garrett, Mrs., of Penge, active voter at 102, 38
If no relatives, spend on poor, 45 [not indexed under Relatives, or Family, or Poor]
Indigestion causing insomnia, 201 [there is no entry for Insomnia]

Norman Douglas

A typical example of Norman Douglas's humour is contained in *Together*, a lively and evocative account of a sojourn in various Austrian mountain villages, first published in 1923. The six-page index is partly a list of proper names, partly a somewhat casual collection of fingerposts for prospective ramblers in Alpine foot-hills; but above all it is a bit of fun, obviously designed to comfort the reader who regrets having come to the end of the text. The index is as informative, colourful and exuberant as the book itself. Here are some typical entries:

Cocoa, an abomination, 10
Fox, as pet, 28; civil behaviour of a, 178
Gluttony, when to be discouraged, 12; when permissible, 13
Grandfather, paternal, a feudal monster, always spick-and-span, 196; excavates in imagination the Akropolis of Athens, 197; tells Prince Consort how to handle Queen Victoria, 198; sometimes mistaken for an angel, 199; dominates his harem, 200; vicious to the last, 201
Hare, how to shoot, 123; how not to cook, 203
Tiefis, village, 33, 40, 48, 69, 98; visit to its tavern, 42; another visit, 126; another, 186; another, 237; destroyed by fire, 126

Douglas also made a collection of limericks, most of them well-known but hitherto confined to repetition in the public bar. It was inevitable in the present permissive age that they should eventually find a publisher.

What makes the book noteworthy is its index. Thus, many readers will know the limerick about The Young Lady of Twickenham; the index heading reads:

Twickenham, unreasonable complaint by female resident of

A. P. Herbert

Sir Alan Herbert in his serious books made his entries straightforward enough, but in his other books the humour springs largely from overstatement and understatement, from alluring, mischievous or satirical descriptions and from the choice of unexpected and unlikely keywords and altogether disarming cross-references.

From his *Misleading Cases in the Common Law* (1927) we have the following gems:

Actresses:
 Appearance of, inappropriate subject for reflection (*see* "Sunday"), 5
Fun:
 No authority for the view that we are here for, 36
 No mention of, in any Act of Parliament, 36
Legal Profession:
 Body and soul, in, difficulty of keeping together, 112
Principle:
 Definitions (*and see* "Blondes"), 91

From his *What a Word!* (1935), these:

Ablative:
 Shameless indifference to the, of Business Man, 66
Advertisers:
 No right to injure English language with barbarous inventions or
 wanton errors, 6, 40, 41, 46, 50, 52, 53, 59, 85, 116, 127
All of Us, So Say:
 Believed not, strictly, correct, 159
Answer is in the Negative, the:
 See "Courtesy"
Australia:
 Believed responsible for birth of "finalize", 60
 Should be watched, 60

Cinema:
    See "Dead Languages"
Commercial English:
    Slump in world-trade, to what extent responsible for, 71, 72, 201
Courtesy:
    The great excuse for circumlocution, 75
English Language:
    Strange neglect of, by bodies and Societies eager to interfere in every
      other human activity, 2, 15, 26, 27, 39

Finally, from his *Bardot M.P.?* (1964):

Authors:
    barbarously used, in life, 99, 100, 107; in death, 81, 84
Cost of Living:
    M.P.'s responsible for inexcusable items in, 71
"Fairness" and "Honesty":
    vividly distinguished, 24

The Stuffed Owl

In 1930 there appeared an anthology of bad verse entitled *The Stuffed Owl*, compiled by D. B. Wyndham-Lewis and Charles Lee. It was confined, as the compilers carefully explained, to good bad verse, as distinct from bad bad verse; an interesting distinction, on which I refer the reader to the book. The works of Dryden, Tennyson and many other poets, some less eminent, give rise to index entries such as these:

Angels, not immune from curiosity, 31, 162; give Mr. Purcell a flying
    lesson, 37; patrol the British sky, 47; invited to take up permanent
    quarters at Whitehall, 50; and Britons, mixed choir of, ibid.
Astronomy, pursuit of, inconsistent with social obligations, 230
Bards, dead, common objects of the sea-shore, 66
Cow, attention drawn to, by Tradition, 8
Eggs, mention of, wrapped in elegant obscurity, 62
England, small but well known, 200; emphatically undegenerate, 202
Fish, Tennyson contrives to avoid mentioning, 247
'Flash! bang!' subtly varied with 'Bang! flash!' (q.v.), 232
George II, his particularly nice virtues, 9; his half-share in the universe, 52;
    his fortunate philoprogenitiveness, 52, 54; his blooming honours, 68;
    his godlike appearance, ibid.
German place-names, the poet does his best with, 54
Italy, not recommended to tourists, 125; examples of what goes on there,
    204, 219, 221

Gordon Carey

When in 1951 Carey's *Making an Index* appeared, the *Times Literary Supplement* reviewer suggested that it might have been better with an index of its own; whereupon the author (with his tongue "in both cheeks") devised an index which contains at least one entry for each letter of the alphabet and is a joy to read. Subtly revised, but just as funny, the index to the third edition (1963) includes the entry:

Jehu (son of Nimshi), 12–13

Wondering what on earth can be the biblical furious driver's connexion with indexing, we hasten to the text, to light upon the following, used as an example:

Nimshison, J., guilty of speeding offences, 97, 102, 111

Another entry reveals the author as a purist:

Horrid word. *See* Alphabetisation

There must also be something to be learnt from the following hilarious entries:

Chase, wild goose. *See* Von Kluck
Goose chase, wild. *See* Kluck, Von
Kluck, von. *See* Von Kluck
Von Kluck. *See* Kluck, von
Wild goose chase. *See* Kluck, von

The Fenian Chief

Robert Collison quoted to me the following amusing entries from the *AB Bookman's Weekly* of June 1968:

Byron, George Gordon Noel, Lord,
    posthumously advises his mistress on playing the stock market, 233
O'Brien, An,
    never turns his back on an enemy, 32
    would never retreat from fields of which ancestors were kings, 33
    does, 34

These entries come from Desmond Ryan's *The Fenian Chief: a biography of James Stephens* (1967), and on turning to the text of the book I found both entries fully justified. Lord Byron's former mistress was the Marquise Teresa Guiccioli, who dabbled in the occult and believed that she received her profitable advice by what we should now call spiritualistic means.

The indexer's sense of humour can be seen in several other entries, such as the following – which, again, accurately reflect the text:

Gill, Peter,
   perjured or perhaps just individualistic, 201
Goldsmith, Rev. John,
   the best of men with a blockhead for a son, 75
Lane, Denny,
   thunderstruck, 176

Unconscious humour

Unconscious, or accidental, humour in an index is usually the result of bad indexing technique. But it can also arise from absurd misreadings of the text, the classic example being the entry about Mr Justice Best, quoted by Wheatley in *How to Make an Index* (p. 157):

Best (Mr Justice), his great mind . . .

This is supposed, says Wheatley, to refer to a passage in the following form:

Mr Justice Best said that he had a great mind to commit the man for trial.

That this joke was already old in Wheatley's day is evident from the fact that he refers to it as hackneyed, and as far as I am aware its origin has never been satisfactorily established.

A modern example of misreading was reported by Mr J. M. Shaftesley in *The Indexer*.[1] It is oddly reminiscent of Carey's joke about "Jehu, son of Nimshi":

[1] "The 'Jewish Chronicle' Index, 1841–", *The Indexer*, Vol. 4, No. 1 (Spring 1964), p. 6.

I remember that for 1857 I had to enter the name of a New York Deputy District Attorney as "Joachim, sen.", as it appeared in the paper. There was no occasion to query this, as the especially American habit of calling people "sen." and "jun." was not uncommon. But in 1859, and later, this turned out to be a gentleman with a name of Scandinavian spelling, Lt.-Col. P. J. Joachimsen, appointed Judge Advocate of the National Guard, and I had to amend my cards accordingly.

Failure to read, not the original text, but the completed index entry, must be the explanation of "O Lord, what boots", which occurs as an entry in the index to an old hymn book. The actual first lines of the hymn referred to are:

O Lord what boots it to recall
The hours of anguish spent . . .

Similarly, in Ira D. Sankey's *Sacred Songs and Solos* there occurs the index entry: "There is a land mine", whereas the hymn in fact begins: "There is a land mine eyes have seen . . ." It is needless to point out that the land mines of World War II were unknown in the days of the evangelists Sankey and Moody.

For more instances of defective technique, with analysis of the faults that led to them, one may consult Wheatley's chapter, "The Bad Indexer"; other writers on indexing have also given interesting examples.

Humorous comments on indexing

Humorous writers have not had a great deal to say about indexing, one of the few exceptions to this rule being Stephen Leacock with "The Perfect Index", in his book, *My Remarkable Uncle and other Sketches* (1942). I particularly like his example of undiscerning indexing of proper names. He gives the name Napoleon with a long string of page references following, then gives the actual references as they appear in the hypothetical text:

Page 17 – " wore his hair like Napoleon"
Page 26 – " in the days of Napoleon"
Page 41 – " as fat as Napoleon"
Page 73 – " not so fat as Napoleon"
Page 109 – "was a regular Napoleon at Ping-pong"
etc.

Serious comments on indexing have sometimes had a humorous

side to them; or perhaps it is the other way round. An example, at all events, is Lord Campbell's famous observation in his *Lives of the Chief Justices* (1857):

> So essential did I consider an index to be to every book, that I proposed to bring a Bill into Parliament to deprive an author who publishes a book without an Index of the privilege of copyright; and moreover to subject him for his offence to a pecuniary penalty.[1]

Taking a more limited view of the importance of indexes, Mrs M. D. Anderson wrote in *The Indexer*:[2]

> The indexer can often do a service to the author and publisher by noting corrections and suggestions for the attention of the "official" proof corrector. I have even known this proof-correcting function of the indexer to be advanced as one of the reasons for having an index at all.

A humble status for the indexer also seems to have been envisaged by Alexander Pope in *A further account of the most deplorable condition of Mr Edmund Curll, Bookseller* ("Instructions to a porter how to find Mr Curll's authors"):[3]

> At the Laundress's, at the Hole in the Wall in Cursitor's Alley, up three pair of stairs, the author of my Church history . . . you may also speak to the gentleman, who lies by him in the flock bed, my Index-maker.

This pamphlet is a sequel to one that describes how Pope supposedly poisoned Curll, and tells how the bookseller,[4] on being to some extent recovered, summons his authors to decide how he may best take his revenge. "Whores and authors must be paid beforehand to put them in good humour", declares the insufferable Curll, distributing largesse to the assembled band; whereupon they offer suggestions as to what should be done to Mr Pope. The historian suggests that they should produce a biography of him,

---

[1] Quoted in Wheatley, *How to Make an Index*, p. 83.

[2] Vol. 3, No. 4 (Autumn 1963), p. 163.

[3] Originally published anonymously, this pamphlet was attributed to Swift and was at one time included in his collected *Works*, but in fact it was written by Pope himself. Later in the pamphlet, Pope refers sardonically to critics' complaints that his translation of the *Iliad* is full of errors.

[4] In the eighteenth century, the distinction between "bookseller" and "publisher" had not developed in its present form.

and the index-maker wickedly declares that there would be nothing to beat an index to his Homer.

Returning to our own times, one can profitably search the pages of *The Indexer* for a number of humorous comments on indexing, and for some humorous verse that I am tempted to quote *in extenso*. The following limerick was published in 1967:[1]

> This indexing Person feels free
> To index the sands of the sea.
>   When they say: It's in vain;
>   You must number each grain!
> A computer can do it, cries he.

In the same issue appeared the ballad whose first stanza I have already quoted on p. 34, and an anonymous poem entitled "Who Burns the Candle":

> Who burns the Candle here, and Toils
>   Amain,
> Scanning the Lines with Busy Eye and
>   Brain,
>   Chasing Elusive Purports with his Pen,
> Pinning them down, and Plodding on
>   again?
>
> The Author's Shadow Self, th'Indexer he,
> His task the Author's Thoughts in Due
>   Degree
>   To Range and Number, and with
>   Watchful Heed
> To make the Author with Himself Agree.
>
> Then comes the Reader asking What?
>   and Where?
> His Road made Ready by th'Indexer's
>   Care;
>   The Flighty Thoughts are Netted,
>   Number'd, Known,
> Like Waterbirds within the Fowler's
>   Snare.
>
> The Hasty Seeker lets the Volume Fall;
> The Index Serves; he need not Read at all.
>   But the Slow Student dwells on every
>   Word,

---

[1] *The Indexer*, Vol. 5, No. 4 (Autumn 1967), p. 206.

The Index too, and finds the Whole too
Small.

When I was acting as Secretary to the Society of Indexers I was asked to tender by return my lowest possible f.o.b. prices for the following, required in Iran:

300—Index, tabbed, size 8½ in. by 6 in. tab of ⅜ in. made from 130 Gr./Sq. M.
Colour: Yellow paper.
Lettering: printed on white paper and covered transparent plastic.
Alphabetical "A–Z".
For MESC General Index Binders.

I ascertained over the telephone that, as I had suspected, the mistake arose through my name appearing under the heading "Indexers" in the *London Yellow Pages* classified telephone directory of trades and professions.

Fortunately, I was able to see the funny side of it.

APPENDIXES

APPENDIX ONE

The Society of Indexers

by J. Ainsworth Gordon, *Secretary, Society of Indexers*

Some people are good at doing things; some have a gift for getting things done. If Norman Knight had not been blessed with both these qualities, it is unlikely that the Society of Indexers would ever have been born. He started book-indexing as a spare-time occupation in the 1920s. Thirty years later, in 1956, he did not know the name of a single other person working in this field. By writing to the press, he established contacts with other indexers. Within less than a year, no fewer than sixty-five fellow workers joined him in inaugurating the Society, at half past ten on the morning of Saturday, 30 March 1957.

Four organizations of particular significance were represented at this birth. The National Book League provided the birthplace, and remains the Society's longest-standing friend and ally. Links with the past were preserved by the British Record Society, which had absorbed the old Index Society in 1890.[1] Aslib enabled the Society to put down firm roots in the various fields of technological development which become increasingly important as time goes by. And the close links between indexers and librarians were endorsed by the Library Association, whose collaboration must count as one of the most potent factors in the Society's successful development.

By March of the following year (1958), the first issue of the Society's journal, *The Indexer*, was in circulation. Twenty-one years and forty-two issues later, it has become a veritable mine of

---

[1] The Index Society, of which Henry Wheatley was the first Secretary, was founded in 1877. Its principal aim was to prepare and publish indexes for books that lacked them. Several indexes and bibliographies were duly published, before lack of funds led to the merger with the British Record Society, whose work in the field of original records was similar.

information about indexing, and has regular subscribers in some sixty countries around the world.

Even earlier, by July 1957, members began meeting together to hear talks by experts on various aspects of indexing, and also to learn from each other by the interchange of ideas and experience. For many years, and for obvious reasons, participation in these meetings was possible only for members living within reach of London, where they were always held. It was not until 1974 that the horizon began to widen, when members on Merseyside held the first meeting of members outside London. This outward spread of activity gained impetus, early in 1976, from the Society's first national conference. This not only brought together members from all parts of the country, but also spurred the members in Scotland to organize the first regional conference, held in Edinburgh in March 1977. Furthermore, the success of the first national conference emboldened the Society to organize another "first" – an international conference in 1978, the twenty-first anniversary year, with representation from all five continents.

In some respects, the speed of developments overseas came as something of a surprise. From the outset, indexers in other countries started to enrol as members, particularly in North America. By 1968, the membership in the United States and Canada had so advanced in numbers and in activities that an independent American Society of Indexers was founded, becoming formally affiliated to the original Society in 1971 and sharing *The Indexer* as official organ. A somewhat similar pattern in Australia reached its climax with the formation, in 1976, of the Australian Society of Indexers, affiliated in 1977 and likewise sharing *The Indexer*. In 1977 the Indexing and Abstracting Society of Canada/ Société canadienne pour l'analyse de documents was founded, and its affiliation was formally approved late in 1978. (On these three societies, see Appendixes 2–4.)

Indexing standards and techniques have always been the Society's primary concern. Its first major impact in this field came in 1964, with the publication of the British Standards Institution's *BS 3700: 1964, Recommendations for the preparation of indexes for books, periodicals, and other publications*, in the preparation of which the Society played a prominent part. (Its index was the personal handiwork of Norman Knight.) This standard has recently been revised to cover subsequent developments and refinements, again with the Society's participation (and this time indexed by L. M. Harrod, for many years Editor of *The Indexer*). The Society has also contributed to the preparation of various other British Standards on topics relevant to indexing, and continues to do so.

Procedures have also been evolved, gradually and with care, for assessing the indexing standards of the Society's own members. These led to the creation, in 1968, of a Register of Indexers; also of a Board of Assessors, whose functions are to establish and monitor standards of indexing competence, and to apply these in adjudicating on applications from members to be admitted to the Register.

One of the most vital problems which confronted the Society's founders was the training of indexers. The only way of becoming a book-indexer was to start as an amateur and learn by experience, but it seemed essential that newcomers to indexing should be enabled to learn from the experience of those who had already learned the hard way. In the spring of 1958 the first steps were taken, when experienced members conducted a series of training discussions, attended by more than forty members. This approach continued until 1961, when the first full-scale ten-lecture course, run entirely by the Society, took place at the North Western Polytechnic in London. Thereafter, a similar course was provided each winter; and in 1969 the substance of the lectures was drawn together by Norman Knight into book form, and published under the title *Training in Indexing*.

The training courses continued until 1971, by which time it became clear that a London-based course was unable to meet the demand for training, not only in many parts of the United Kingdom but also in a number of overseas countries. It was necessary to find a way of making training facilities available to anyone, anywhere, at any time; clearly, the only possible answer was a correspondence course, though this was something the Society had no means of providing. That is how it came about that the only universally accessible course in book-indexing is provided by a private-enterprise correspondence college. In 1973 the Rapid Results College included in its prospectus a course in the principles and techniques of indexing, written by one of the Society's most experienced members, which has since enabled over 500 widely scattered neophytes to learn the elements of indexing.

Though the purpose of the founders was to create a professional body, and not a trade union or an employment agency, the re-muneration of indexers has inevitably been of great interest to the Society. So too have such matters as the contractual relationships between indexers and publishers, copyright and royalties, and the general status of indexers. These are fields in which progress can rarely be recorded in terms of dates and events; if it could be shown as a graph, the line would slope gently upwards, slightly undulating but devoid of dramatic mountains and valleys. The world of publishing is so multifarious and so fragmented, even when allowance is made for the unifying influence of the Pub-lishers' Association, that there is no general front on which progress can be made; and the Society has learned to work patiently and persistently from the particular to the general.

Little has been said, in this brief history, of technological developments in indexing, primarily because their application to book-indexing is still very much in the exploratory stage; and it is book-indexing which has been the Society's main concern, and will continue to be as long as books and periodicals are published with sub-standard indexes, and even without indexes at all. Meanwhile, an increasing number of people engaged in other types of indexing can be found among the members, and – as is evident from the content of *The Indexer* – the Society caters also for their particular interests.

The Society now continues without the wise leadership of its founder. While this book was in production, Norman Knight died shortly before reaching his eighty-seventh birthday. Deeply though his loss is felt, he leaves behind a firmly rooted and mature organi-zation. "You all know," he said, towards the end of his days, "that the Society of Indexers is the apple of my eye." Its members are impelled, by the example of his total commitment, not merely to maintain the traditions and principles that he did so much to establish, but to scale new heights of achievement.

APPENDIX TWO

The American Society of Indexers (ASI)

by Alan R. Greengrass

It ought to be easy to write about the founding of a society less than ten years old. The participants have not dispersed too far and memories should not have grown too dim. But somehow it is not easy to pinpoint exactly how the American Society of Indexers came into being. Even though we all should have known it was history in the making, the details have begun to fade.

I was present at the creation, more or less as an innocent bystander. The year was 1968 and I was finishing up my library school degree at Columbia University. I had originally been lured (and perhaps shoved a bit) into pursuing a library degree by Dr Theodore C. Hines – and it was in and around his office in Columbia's Butler Library that the American Society of Indexers was first conceived.

At this point, things become a bit hazy. Dr Hines is the sort of professor who communicates his enthusiasm for, and fascination with, indexing to those around him. While it is not clear exactly who said what to whom, everyone agrees that Mary Flad, a student of Dr Hines', expressed the feeling that people interested in practical indexing had no professional organization to call their own and volunteered to help organize a meeting of interested persons. (Ironically, Ms Flad moved away from the New York area shortly thereafter and has never actually participated in ASI.)

Ted Hines and Mary Flad were not the only ones who felt the need for an organization concerned with the full range of indexing practices and problems. A press release announcing the formation of an indexing society was published in several library and book trade periodicals; that was really the extent of the initial membership drive. The response was gratifying. By February 1969 prior to ASI's first formal meeting, there were already 112 members.

Robert J. Palmer, who had previously served as corresponding member from the United States to the British Society, became ASI's liaison with the Society of Indexers and immediately began studying the possibility of formal affiliation between the two societies. Mr Palmer was also chief architect of the ASI constitution.

Other people who worked actively on behalf of ASI during its infancy included Dee Atkinson, John Fall, Marlene Hurst, George Lowy, Anne Richter and Dr John Rothman. At the founding meeting, I was chosen President *pro tem* (youth and inexperience apparently being prime qualifications) and Dr Jessica L. Harris was chosen Secretary–Treasurer *pro tem*.

The first annual general meeting was held on 16 June 1969 at the New York City University Graduate Center. Dr Charles Bernier was elected President of the fledgling society and Eleanor Steiner-Prag was elected Vice President. The constitution was approved overwhelmingly and committees were established.

The American Society of Indexers has evolved in many directions since then. Affiliation between the British and American societies was formally ratified in 1971 and *The Indexer* became ASI's official journal. Evening meetings turned into all-day meetings. While New York has remained the center of ASI activities, the current membership of well over 300 is widely distributed geographically. The 1976 annual meeting was held in Chicago and the 1978 meeting in Washington, DC.

Under Presidents Charles Bernier, Eleanor Steiner-Prag, John Fall, Barbara Preschel, Mary Lee Tsuffis and BevAnne Ross, ASI has made some very tangible contributions to the profession. Standards and guidelines have been published, a register of members available for freelance assignments is distributed annually to leading publishers, a *Directory of Courses on Indexing in Canada and the United States* has been compiled and a start has been made in studying the murky subject of indexer economics.

ASI's most significant contribution, however, is something more difficult to itemize or measure. For the first time, American freelance indexers and others concerned with indexing as an intellectual discipline and as a profession (albeit an often invisible one) have an organization devoted to their interests and needs.

ASI meetings have served as a forum where indexers could exchange ideas, compare problems and argue over priorities. The end result, I think, is that indexers are a little more visible than they once were and have developed a greater sense of professional standing.

At the beginning of its constitution, ASI states the following objectives:

1) to improve the quality of indexing and to secure useful standards for the field;

2) to act as an advisory body on the qualification and remuneration of indexers to which authors, editors, publishers and others may apply for guidance;

3) to issue from time to time books, articles, and other material on the subject of indexing and to cooperate with other societies and organizations in such publication;

4) to defend and safeguard the professional interests of indexers;

5) to cooperate with other societies and organizations in the field of indexing and information science and especially with The Society of Indexers (Great Britain).

That was why ASI was founded. I think the growing pains have been worthwhile.

APPENDIX THREE

The Australian Society of Indexers

by Clyde Garrow, *President, Australian Society of Indexers,* and
Jean Hagger, *Secretary, Australian Society of Indexers*

The evolution of the Australian Society of Indexers is a long and
rather strange story. The first seeds were sown, not by an Australian, but by an Englishman who made his career in the London
office of the Bank of Adelaide. During the last two years of his
life, Alfred T. H. Talbot devoted himself, as the Membership
Secretary of the Society of Indexers, to building up the young
society and, in the year before his death in 1960, he had the
inspiration of inviting the daughter of a former bank colleague to
become corresponding member for Australia. Thus it was that
Brenda Miller became, for the next decade, the link between
indexers in Australia and England.

During the late 1960s, she made the acquaintance of a fellow
member, H. Godfrey Green, who was not only a practising indexer
but also thought it possible, by mounting a membership drive, to
build up an Australian branch of the Society. On Brenda Miller's
suggestion, he became the corresponding member in Australia.

Even before the Society had confirmed his formal appointment
in this position (16 May 1972), his recruiting drive was already
launched. Within six months, when the membership had risen to
about 30, a general meeting drew up and adopted a constitution
for The Society of Indexers in Australia. Approval for the use of
this formal title was sought from and given by the Society's
Council in London the following April.

Membership grew to approximately 100; meetings were held;
newsletters were published; Australian members not only read
The Indexer but wrote articles for it.

In September 1975, the whole scene changed. Godfrey Green

found that changes in domestic circumstances deprived him of the time and opportunity to continue in office. Jean Uhl, assisted by Dorothy Prescott and Henry Thorburn, gallantly agreed to take over the reins, and quickly called a meeting of all the members who were interested and available. An interim committee was formed to prepare the ground for inaugurating a new organization to be built on the foundations of the existing one.

On 27 April 1976, the last general meeting of the Society of Indexers in Australia, having approved the termination of that organization's existence, became the inaugural meeting of the Australian Society of Indexers, the world's third society of indexers.

It is a vigorous society. It has established cordial relations with the original Society in Great Britain and with the American Society, and has negotiated terms of affiliation with the British Society. By December 1976 it had published its first newsletter. It is planning to establish a Register of Indexers, somewhat similar in character and operation to that of the "parent" society.

Already the new society's programmes of meetings have considered many facets of indexing from the traditional book index through to the indexing techniques used in the computer-readable systems. Some discussion of indexing theory has been introduced and future programmes will continue to expose members to a wide spectrum of indexing practice and theory. The Australian Society of Indexers looks forward with enthusiasm and some excitement.

The Indexing and Abstracting Society of Canada/Société canadienne pour l'analyse de documents

by Peter E. Greig, *Past President, Indexing and Abstracting Society of Canada*

The establishment of an Index Committee by the Bibliographical Society of Canada in 1969 marked the first effort to provide a forum for indexers in Canada. The objectives of this committee were to maintain indexes to the Society's publications and to related publications, to act as a clearing-house for index projects, to promote index production and to publicize developments in indexing. Despite the interest and support of Society members, and the publication of an occasional newsletter, the committee was unable to provide a comprehensive programme in answer to the needs of Canadian indexers, or to attract the national support of indexers in a country as large as Canada. In 1973 the committee was replaced by the appointment of an Indexer to the Bibliographical Society of Canada who continues to maintain the Society's commitment to the above objectives.

In March 1977 the Committee on Bibliographical Services for Canada (CBSC), a committee of the National Library Advisory Board, convened the Canadian Abstracting and Indexing Services Workshop in the National Library of Canada. The participants at the workshop, including representatives from eighteen Canadian abstracting and indexing services, noted the absence of a specific forum for abstracters and indexers in Canada. One of the recommendations of the workshop was that an association be formed in answer to this need.

The members of the CBSC felt that such an association could

only be established by those persons most concerned. The CBSC sponsored an Open Forum for Indexers and Abstracters on 12 June 1977 at the Annual Conference of the Canadian Library Association in Montreal. Six hundred invitations were sent to individual abstracters and indexers, A & I services, libraries and publishers across Canada. This meeting resulted in the establishment of the Indexing and Abstracting Society of Canada/Société canadienne pour l'analyse de documents (IASC/SCAD).

Participants at the meeting volunteered to form a temporary executive committee, to draft a constitution and to undertake the administrative work necessary to any new association. The Secretariat of the CBSC has provided a mailing address and secretarial services during the IASC's initial year. The temporary executive of the IASC immediately circulated the minutes of the Montreal meeting, with a draft constitution and a questionnaire, to those persons who had expressed interest in the Society. The replies to this questionnaire affirmed the general objectives of the IASC, as expressed in the draft constitution, and appointed a permanent executive until elections could be held in May 1978.

The general objectives of the IASC are to encourage the production and use of indexes and abstracts, to promote workshops for users of A & I services, to promote the recognition of indexers and abstracters, to improve indexing and abstracting techniques and to increase communication among individuals involved in indexing and abstracting in Canada. The executive consists of a president, a vice-president, a secretary, a treasurer, an editor and six regional directors.

The Society issues the *IASC/SCAD Newsletter*, begun in February 1978, on an occasional basis. In addition to professional news and information of interest to members of the Society, the newsletter contains a continuing bibliography of current materials on indexing and abstracting. The 1978 annual meeting of the IASC, held in Edmonton, Alberta, was the occasion for a one-day national conference on indexing and abstracting, and the state of the art in Canada. The Society intends to continue holding annual national meetings on this model. A number of regional groups have been and are being formed, each with its own regional programme of activity. Terms of affiliation between the Society of Indexers and the IASC were approved by the two societies late in 1978.

The Wheatley Medal

by K. G. B. Bakewell, *Chairman, Society of Indexers*

In 1960 the Library Association instituted the Wheatley Medal, an annual award to the compiler of the most outstanding index first published in Britain during the preceding year. In 1968, following a joint meeting of the Society of Indexers and the Library Association Cataloguing and Indexing Group, the conditions of the award were modified, one of the changes being that indexes published during the preceding three years would be eligible, in recognition of the fact that an index can only be judged by its performance over a reasonable period. The current conditions may be obtained from the Library Association.

The medal was named after Henry B. Wheatley (1838–1917), who wrote several books on indexing and related subjects and is sometimes referred to as "the father of British indexing". The major purpose of the award was to make publishers more aware of the importance of an index to any non-fiction work.

The award is chosen by a panel consisting of three nominees of the Library Association and three nominees of the Society of Indexers. It says much for the high standards expected for the Medal – and perhaps something for the poor quality of indexes in those days – that no award was made for the first two years. The first winner was Michael Maclagan in 1962, and he was the first of five author-indexers to receive the award.

WINNERS OF THE WHEATLEY MEDAL

1960 (No award)
1961 (No award)
1962 Michael Maclagan   Michael Maclagan, *"Clemency" Canning* (Macmillan)

1963 J. M. Dickie	J. M. Dickie, *How to catch trout* (W. & R. Chambers)
1964 Guy Parsloe	Guy Parsloe, *Wardens' accounts of the Worshipful Company of the Founders of the City of London 1497–1681* (University of London, Athlone Press)
1965 Alison M. Quinn	Richard Hakluyt, *The principall navigations voiages and discoveries of the English nation* (Cambridge University Press/Hakluyt Society and Peabody Museum of Salem)
1966 (No award)	
1967 G. Norman Knight	Randolph S. Churchill, *Winston S. Churchill*, Vol. 2, *Young statesman 1901–1919* (Heinemann)
1968 Doreen Blake and Ruth Bowden	Cumulative index, *Journal of Anatomy 1866–1966* (Cambridge University Press/Anatomical Society)
1969 James C. Thornton	M. House and G. Storey (eds), *The letters of Charles Dickens*, Vol. 2, *1840–41* (Oxford: The Clarendon Press)
1970 E. L. C. Mullins	E. L. C. Mullins, *A guide to the historical & archaeological publications of societies in England & Wales 1901–1933* (University of London, Athlone Press)
1971 (No award)	
1972 (No award)	
1973 K. Boodson	K. Boodson, *Non-ferrous metals: a bibliographical guide* (Macdonald Technical & Scientific)
and L. M. Harrod	H. M. Colvin (ed.), *History of the King's works*, Vol. 6, *1782–1851* (HMSO)
1974 C. C. Banwell	*Encyclopedia of forms & precedents*, 4th edn, 24 vols (Butterworth)

1975 Margaret D. Anderson   Judith Butcher, *Copy-editing: the Cambridge handbook* (Cambridge University Press)

1976 John A. Vickers   G. R. Cragg, *The works of John Wesley*, Vol. II, *The appeals to men of reason and religion and certain related open letters* (Oxford University Press)

1977 T. Rowland Powel   *Archaeologia Cambrensis*, 1901–1960 (Cardiff: Cambrian Archaeological Association)

1978 (No Award)

APPENDIX SIX

The Carey Award

by K. G. B. Bakewell, *Chairman, Society of Indexers*

In 1977 the Society of Indexers established a new occasional award for outstanding services to indexing, designated the Carey Award in memory of the Society's first President, Gordon V. Carey (1886–1969). Carey was a man of many parts: boy chorister at King's College, rugger blue, Cambridge don, headmaster of Eastbourne College, executive of the Cambridge University Press, author and librarian, and a man who had served his country with distinction throughout both world wars. He also had a passion for the art of indexing, about which he wrote a number of books and articles, and in 1957 he was one of the founder members of the Society of Indexers. He was described by an anonymous reviewer in *The Times Literary Supplement* as "The Prince of Indexers".

The first recipient of the Carey Award, an appropriately worded and beautifully illuminated framed parchment, was the founder and then President of the Society of Indexers, G. Norman Knight.

INDEX

by G. Norman Knight and Anthony Raven

A. R. writes: Norman Knight originally intended to index this book himself, but in the spring of 1978 he invited me to assist him. At that time he was able to write only with difficulty, and very slowly. The intention was that he would mark the text, I would write the cards, and he would edit them. He began by marking the greater part of a copy of the typescript, but he died in the summer when the first proofs of the book were still awaited. In completing the index I have endeavoured to follow his preferences in optional matters, though I may have departed from that principle in some respects. It will be clear that the author is not responsible for any shortcomings of the index, or for any discrepancies between the precepts of his text and my own practice.

Scope of the index
The Foreword and Appendixes have been indexed, but not the author's Preface.

The Indexer, Training in Indexing, and other publications have not been indexed when they are merely named as the source of something in the text.

Alphabetical arrangement
This is word-by-word. (For an explanation of that expression, see pp. 121–2.)

A single letter in an abbreviation or proper name has been treated as a single word ("q.v." precedes "qualifications").

Abbreviations have been indexed according to the abbreviated spelling ("Mr" follows "Montaigne").

Hyphened expressions have been treated as single words when the first element is a prefix that cannot ordinarily stand alone, otherwise as two words ("sub-subheadings" follows "subject headings").

Prepositions etc. at the beginning of subheadings have been ignored in determining the alphabetical order of subheadings, with the exception of "not" which has been treated as a keyword and indexed under N.

Special usages

above and *below* in cross-references indicate that the reference is to another subheading under the same heading, not to a separate heading.

"quoted" in a personal name heading indicates quotation on some subject not directly pertaining to indexing. Where the subject-matter of a quotation or statement in the text does pertain to indexing, it is usually indicated by a modification or subheading, no attempt being made to distinguish direct from indirect speech.

The letters "n." and "e." immediately following page references indicate footnotes and epigraphs respectively.

bis or *ter*, immediately following a page reference, indicates that there are two, or three, separate references to the subject on the page.

Words in brackets immediately following a page reference are intended to locate the reference, in a case where the subject of the heading or subheading is not explicitly mentioned in the text. (These bracketed words are not intended to do more than locate the reference; unlike modifications and subheadings, they do not necessarily indicate the subject-matter.)